By-Way
Travels
South of London

Geoff Marshall

Published by Sigma Leisure – an imprint of
Sigma Press, 1 South Oak Lane, Wilmslow, Cheshire SK9 6AR, England.

British Library Cataloguing in Publication Data
A CIP record for this book is available from the British Library.

ISBN: 1-85058-377-3

Typesetting and Design by: Sigma Press, Wilmslow, Cheshire.

Text photographs: the author

Cover: Colin Curbishley

Printed and bound by: Manchester Free Press

General Disclaimer

Whilst every effort has been made to ensure that the information given in this book is correct, neither the publisher nor the author accept any responsibility for any inaccuracy.

PREFACE

By Way Travels South of London consists of twelve chapters based on routes for the cyclist, (or motorist), all within one hour of London. A description is given of places of historic and architectural interest found in both village and countryside off the beaten track.

The unique feature of "By Way Travels" is that, whereas in other publications, busy and congested main roads tend to be used, in this case all the routes are along little-known and quiet country lanes. It was decided to keep them as close as possible to London and in every case they are within one hour of the capital. In this way, a very large number of people can have ready access to the peace and tranquillity found so close to London, and enjoy the abundance of history and architecture found along the way. A full description of the route is given at the end of each chapter with Ordnance Survey references to help.

The directions for most of the routes start at motorway intersections. This has only been done for convenience and as a way of directing you to the starting point proper of each route which is point "A", the first place of interest. Thus, the first part of each route is often on point "A" from whichever direction is convenient to you. The more detailed instructions are really for the motorist and because point A may be remotely located and therefore difficult to find.

As emphasised before, as a high priority, the routes are all along quiet country lanes. Inevitably, however, there are sections on main roads but these have been kept to the absolute minimum. The routes are therefore particularly suitable for cyclists. They have also been kept deliberately close to London.

A point worth mentioning is that throughout the book there are descriptions of private houses, not open to the public. Pevsner, in *The Building of England* series, deals with this with a phrase such as "mention of a house in this volume does not necessarily mean that it is open to the public". The same goes for "By Way Travels".

There are SAFETY aspects which I think should be highlighted. The first is that the route should not be worked out while driving or cycling along. This can be very dangerous, particularly for motorists, because it distracts from proper attention to the road and to other traffic. It is best that at each stopping point, e.g. B, the next section should be worked out, i.e. B – C. A good navigator helps, of course. Many of the lanes used are really very remote (particularly in Kent, on the Downs) and narrow, with passing places and cars can be rare. Other lanes are not quite so remote but even on quiet lanes, for the most part free of traffic, a car can appear at speed round a blind corner and so cyclists should take special care at all times.

It may be of some interest to know how the book was conceived. Ever since I came to live in the London area, I have been keenly interested in London itself and have spent much time wandering round the place and getting to know it. Every year, millions of tourists descend and I have observed them being herded around the sights by motor coach. It seems to me that they never see the countryside! And when they do leave London they troop off in the coach along the M40 motorway to Stratford, or the M2 to Canterbury. By the weary expressions on many of their faces I rather feel they would much prefer to perhaps hire a car and go off exploring on their own and at their own pace. "By Way Travels" meets their needs – all of the routes are within one hour of the capital and there is also a feel for the real England rather than tourist towns. In addition, local residents in the Greater London area and the South East of England number many millions and "By Way Travels" is an excellent way to get to know what is on the doorstep.

The book is not exhaustive in the area it covers. I have selected what I consider to be the most interesting and attractive aspects of the countryside close to and south of London. The book most definitively deals with off-the-beaten-track places and (with the possible exceptions of Wisley Garden) excludes well-known tourist attractions like Chart-well, Hever Castle and Knole. It also excludes towns in areas such as Dorking or Sevenoaks.

I hope you get as much enjoyment from your explorations as I have from mine.

Finally, I would like to dedicate this book to all my family.

Geoff Marshall

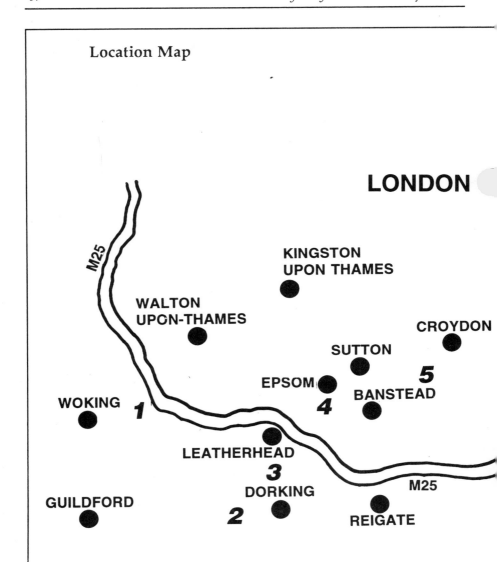

Location Map

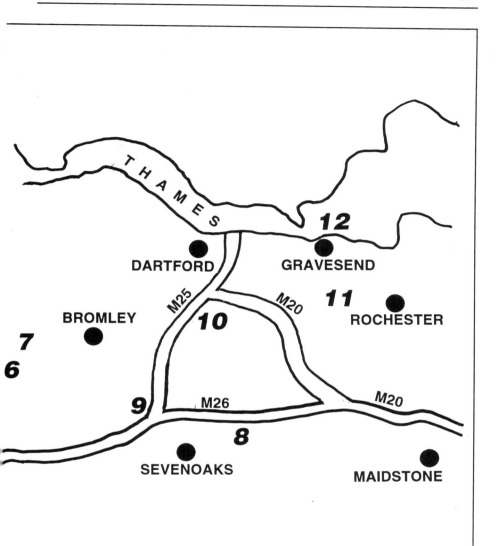

CONTENTS

1: Rock Gardens, Rose Gardens and Dr Invincible

Route: Wisley – Pyrford – East Clandon – Silent Pool – West Horsley – Ockham

Distance: 27 miles/43 km

Wisley

Wisley is famous for housing the gardens of the Royal Horticultural Society. The gardens were originally started by the then Treasurer, G.F. Wilson, in 1878. After his death, the garden passed to Sir Thomas Hanbury, who donated it to the Society "for the purpose of an experimental garden and the encouragement and improvement of scientific and practical horticulture in all its branches". Originally in Chiswick, the garden moved to Wisley in 1904 and now consists of 200 glorious acres of every sort and description, from rock gardens to rose gardens, and formal gardens to fruit gardens.

Further along the lane is the original village of Wisley. The mediaeval group of diminutive church and 16th century timber-framed farmhouse is much praised for retaining its rural setting and atmosphere while being so close to Byfleet. You can get the feel of this as you look at the group from the lane. And yet what a contrast is found by turning through 180 degrees to witness the roar of the M25, now just a few hundred yards away.

The church is entered through a 17th century timber porch enclosing a Norman door. The chancel arch is Norman and there are 12th century windows on the north and south side of the chancel. The building has a queen post roof.

Further along the lane is the Wey Navigation Canal. It was Sir Richard Weston of nearby Sutton Place who employed 200 men to construct the canal, which opened in 1653. The cost was £15,000, but an annual income of £1,500 assured the success of the project. The canal joined Guildford with the River Thames and it was eventually extended to Godalming in 1762. Grain, wool and timber were carried to London and it is recorded that in 1664, 4000 barge-loads of timber passed along it.

Pyrford

The church at Pyrford, and its situation, is perfectly described by Sir Thomas Jackson, who restored it in 1869: "Humble and modest as the

It is said that Thomas Cromwell bombarded Newark Priory from Church Hill in 1539 at the time of the Dissolution of the Monasteries.

Painting in porch of Pyrford Church

building is, it has always seemed to me the very model of a small English church. Nothing could be happier than the site that has been chosen for it, on the brow of a steep bank overlooking the broad meadows through which the river Wey winds, with Newark Priory in the middle distance and the chalk hills beyond."

The church is entered through the 16th century north porch, where there is a pictorial history describing Pyrford and its church through the ages. There is much small-scale Norman architectural detail. The north door has zig-zag moulding and there are two Norman windows at the west end of the nave, on either side of the buttress. The north wall of the chancel also has a Norman window and there is a plain Norman chancel arch. There is an attractive pulpit of 1628, complete with tester.

Further down the road towards Ripley we pass the picturesque ruins of Newark Priory standing alone in a meadow. There are notices saying that the field in which it stands is private, and so all that can be really appreciated is the distant view of the ruined south transept and chancel of the 13th century church. The Priory was founded in 1190 by Augustinian canons and is quoted in Gilbert White's "Natural History of Selbourne" as being the haunt of jackdaws.

East Clandon

The showpiece of East Clandon, a pleasant village set back from the main road, is Hatchlands, a Palladian house built in 1757 for Admiral Edward Boscawen. The name Clandon derives from the Anglo-Saxon "Cleane Dun" (clean down) and the village lies on cultivatable land between the clay to the north and the chalk downs to the south. The church is dedicated to St. Thomas of Canterbury and, as such, is unique in Surrey.

Hatchlands

Hatchlands is approached down a lane to the east of the village. Admiral Boscawen played a distinguished part in the 7-year war and won a famous victory over the French fleet in 1758 at Cape Breton, Canada. He was later in command of the fleet in the Mediterranean and, by defeating a number of French ships, prevented them from concentrating around Brest for an invasion of Great Britain. He is buried far away at St. Michael Pentevil in Cornwall, where his epitaph tells how Hatchlands was built "at the expense of the enemies of this country" – in other words, with prize money from the French wars. The house is notable for being the first commission of the 30-year-old Robert Adam after he returned from Italy and Dalmatia. Joseph Bonomi made alterations to the house in 1790. It then passed through various hands before being donated to the National Trust in 1945.

Silent Pool

The Silent Pool is one of Surrey's famous beauty spots. In fact, there are two ponds: the upper and the lower. They were formerly known as Shireburn Ponds, and are surrounded with legend. Martin Tupper, a notable figure in these parts in the 19th century, wrote the historical novel 'Stephan Langton' in which King John surprises the beautiful daughter of a woodcutter while she is bathing in the pool. The story then goes that she ran away and in doing so fell into the water and drowned. Drowned also was her brother, who tried to rescue her. They can both still be seen when the moon is full at midnight!

West Horsley

West Horsley used to be known as Horsley Green. The developed village now lies to the west of the 13th century church of St. Mary and the nearby West Horsley Place. The substantial church has a flint west tower with a door of c1200 and a handsome shingled spire. The three-light east window contains two good 13th century stained glass medallions in the north and central lancet. To the north is an angel rescuing St. Catherine from the torture of the wheel, and in the centre Mary Magdalene at the feet of Christ.

The Nicholas chapel to the south now houses the organ. It is not particularly accessible but is renowned for being the burial place of the

Silent Pool

head of Sir Walter Raleigh. Raleigh was executed in 1618 and his widow preserved his severed head in a red leather bag for more than 25 years. Raleigh's son, Carew, lived at West Horsley Place, and the story goes that the head was finally buried in the south chapel of the church.

West Horsley Place is a few hundred yards away to the north of the church. It dates from 1630, has a 10-bay brick south front with pediment and Dutch gable. The house later passed to the Nicholas family. During a storm in 1703, a falling chimney killed the wife of Sir John Nicholas. It is said that her son, William, saw the head of Raleigh at his mother's burial!

Just for the record, Sir Walter Raleigh's body is buried either at Beddington, near Croydon, or St Margaret's, Westminster.

Ockham

The stamp of the Lovelace family is evident at Ockham. They owned Ockham Park in the mid-nineteenth century and were responsible for building the estate cottages and buildings that abound in the village.

The church is usually locked, but the key can be obtained from the Post Office and the effort is worthwhile. The most distinguished feature of the church is its 13th century east window of seven lancets. The window has dog-tooth moulding on the arches and shafts of Petworth marble. There is a possibility that the window may originally have been at nearby Newark Priory and then re-set at Ockham at the Dissolution in 1536. The window is splendid and unique in the country, apart from another example at Blakeney in Norfolk and a Victorian window at Millbrook in Southampton.

An interesting piece of graffiti can be found on one of the panes of glass in the south-west window of the chancel. Here is written: "W. Peten new leaded this in 1775 and was never paid for this same".

Ockham's most notable former resident was William of Occam, who is said to have been born here in 1280 when Ralph de Malling was Rector. William grew up to be the famous philosopher – Doctor Invincible. He joined the Franciscan Order and studied at the University of Oxford in 1310. He was a nominalist, which I am told means that he believed that universals do not exist – or the existence of a general word does not imply the existence of a general thing named by it. Heady stuff for the Surrey countryside. One of his dictums is known as 'Occam's Razor': "Entities should not be multiplied beyond what is necessary", or in other words "don't adopt a complicated explanation if a simple one will do".

William Ockham held that God could only be known by faith and not by reason – a view at variance with that of Thomas Aquinas. He was summoned to the Papal Court at Avignon to answer for his views, but he escaped to Munich where, under the protection of Louis of Bavaria, he spent the rest of his life.

William Ockham was one of the most eminent men of his day and is held by many to be a forerunner of Martin Luther.

ROUTE

➠ From the M25 (Junction 10) proceed on the A3 towards Guildford. After 1.6 miles leave at the first exit (B2039) and retrace steps back to A3 following the signs for R.H.S. Wisley Garden. Leave the A3 after 0.6 miles and turn left (signposted Wisley RHS Garden). After 0.2 miles turn left for Wisley Garden (066583) (A).

➠ **CYCLISTS: route starts here**

➠ Continue along the lane for 1.2 miles to Wisley Church (056596) (B).

➠ Continue for 0.5 miles to Wey navigation canal (053593) (C).

➠ Continue for 0.4 miles and turn left into Pyrford Road (signposted Ripley). Continue, and after 1.1 miles turn right. After a few yards turn left for Pyrford church (040583) (D).

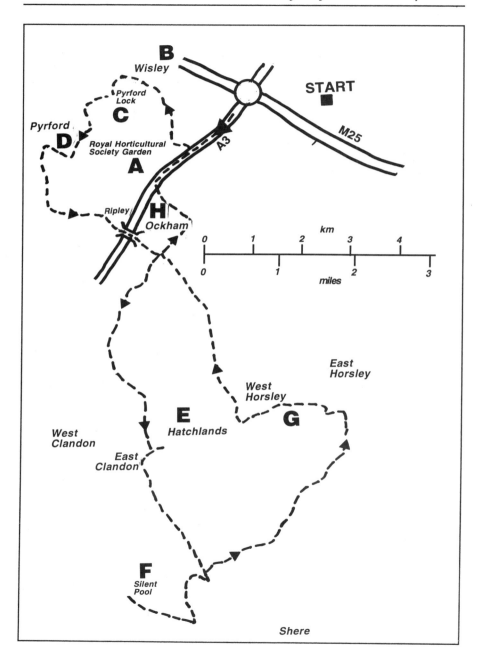

➠Turn right out of Pyrford church and continue for 1.7 miles to Ripley (crossing the River Wey and passing Newark Priory). Turn left at Ripley and first right into Rose Lane. Take second right after 0.9 miles (Hungry Hill Lane). Continue for 3 miles to East Clandon and turn left for Hatchlands (063518) (E).

➠Retrace steps from Hatchlands, pass the church and pub and cross the A246 and proceed towards Shere. After 1.8 miles, turn right and then, after 0.8 miles, turn right onto the A25. After 0.6 miles, turn right and retrace steps for 200 yards to the Silent Pool (060486) (F).

➠Continue for 0.6 miles and turn left (signposted East Clandon, East Horsley and Effingham). After 0.8 miles, turn right (signposted East and West Horsley). Keep right at the first junction (signposted East Horsley) and continue for 3 miles to join A246. Turn left on to A246 (passing Thatchers Hotel) and continue for 0.8 miles to car park on left at West Horsley church (088527) (G).

➠Continue along A246 to first roundabout (by garage) and turn right (signposted Ripley and West Horsley). After 0.2 miles turn left into Ripley Lane. In 2.3 miles take the first right into Guileshill Lane and continue for 0.7 miles, where you turn sharp left for Ockham Church (067566) (H).

➠Turn left from Ockham church to A3 where you turn right for London and the M25.

REFRESHMENTS

1. Tea Rooms within Wisley Gardens (066583)

2. The Anchor – on the Wey Navigation Canal between Wisley and Pyrford (054594)

3. The Seven Stars – between Pyrford and Ripley (040570)

4. The Ship (and others) – in Ripley High Street (053567)

5. The Queens Head – East Clandon (059517)

6. Thatchers Hotel – on A246 in East Horsley (096526)

7. The Duke of Wellington – at junction of A246 and B2039 in East Horsley (095527)

2: Abinger Pits and Romans on the Heath

Route: Abinger – Abinger Hammer – Holmbury St. Mary – Ewhurst – Farley Heath – Albury – Shere

Distance: 32 miles/51 km

Abinger

The parish of Abinger is long and narrow, extending 9 miles in a north/south direction but only one mile east/west. There are two distinct centres: Abinger Hatch and Abinger Hammer.

Abinger Hatch is set amid beautiful Surrey scenery and is rich in history. Although Norman, the church is clean and modern-looking. It fell victim to a bomb in the war and was later damaged by fire in 1964. Frederick Etchells restored the church in 1951. There is an excellent modern east window, dated 1967, by Lawrence Lee, depicting Life Through Death. Lee was also responsible for stained glass in Coventry Cathedral. The mediaeval period is represented by a delicate 15th century crucifixion in the south porch.

In most places it is usual for the church to be the site of greatest antiquity, but this is not so in Abinger. Behind the church, in the garden of Abinger Manor House, there is a large Norman motte – but that is not all. Abinger was known to the people of the Mesolithic period. For 5,000 years between the end of the Ice Age (c8300 BC) and the time of the first farmers (3200 BC) small groups of people travelled throughout the land hunting deer and fishing. They lived in temporary pit dwellings and one of these is preserved in a nearby field. It is housed in a small museum in the safe hands of the owners of Abinger Manor Farm. The key can be

obtained from there and all donations are sent to the Red Cross. The site
was excavated in 1950 by Dr. Louis Leakey and the pit dwellings show
the remains of post holes and a hearth. In addition, there is a display of
flint implements, such as blades, axes, knives and so on.

Abinger Hammer

Crossways Farm – the 17th century building mentioned in George
Meredith's "Diana of the Crossways" – is passed at the corner of the
main A25, and then we come to Abinger Hammer. Here, in Elizabethan
times, was a centre of the Wealden iron industry. Abinger Hammer, as
the name implies, is evocative of the former hammer ponds. These were
man-made lakes formed by damming the Tillingbourne stream which
runs through the valley here. A head of water was thereby created
which provided the power to drive the bellows and hammers of the
mediaeval industry. The iron was used in Tudor war ships and also, it is
said, for the gates of Temple Bar. All this, of course, is now gone, for the
industry died during the 18th century, but the ponds remain and are
now watercress beds.

The well-known clock at Abinger Hammer is another reminder of the
bygone industry. It is known as "Jack the Smith" and shows the
blacksmith striking the hour with a hammer. Dated 1891, it has the
inscription: "By me you know how fast to go". It is well worth the wait
to see the clock in action.

Holmbury St. Mary

"It is heaven's gate", so exclaimed the wife of the eminent Victorian
architect, G.E. Street, as they both rode in a carriage in these parts in
1872. Street, renowned for being the designer of the Law Courts in the
Strand, then decided to live here and built the grand 19th century house,
Holmdale, where he was to remain for the rest of his life. His wife died,
as did his second wife a short while afterwards, and it is to the memory
of his second wife that he built the church at his own expense.
Holmbury St. Mary thus came into existence in 1879. The church is
majestically Victorian. There is a tablet at its west end in the narthex, put
there by Street to ensure that seats in the church were free. Indeed, when
Gladstone and his cabinet were at Holmbury St. Mary in 1880, there was

Jack the Smith, Abinger Hammer

no question of their occupying reserved seats and they had to take their places with the rest of the villagers, just as Street had intended.

The church is beautifully adorned. In the chancel there is a 14th century Florentine painting by Spinello Aretino. The view from the church porch looking down the valley is quite splendid.

The area around Holmbury St. Mary, being about half-way between the Sussex coast and London, was a smuggling centre in Napoleonic times. Goods were stored here ready for off-loading in London. The story goes that when local people discovered contraband, they marked some of it with a white cross. This was a signal to the smugglers to indicate that they would not report them to the authorities in return for leaving the crossed items as gifts.

Nearby Holmbury Hill is 857ft high. There is an Iron Age hill fort at its summit which extends to 8 acres. It was occupied by the Celts between 150 BC and 50 AD.

Holmbury St Mary

Ewhurst

Ewhurst is a large and straggling village to the south of Coneyhurst Hill, or Pitch Hill as it is sometimes called. The name Ewhurst means "yew wood".

Ewhurst was familiar to William Cobbett, who complained in his Rural Rides about the well-known wealden clay: "From Ewhurst the first three miles was the deepest clay that I ever saw, to the best of my recollection. I was warned of the difficulty of getting along; but I was not to be frightened by the sound of clay. It took me, however, a good hour and a half to get along these three miles."

Ewhurst has a fine church. Cobbett knew it and wrote: "At Ewhurst, which is a very pretty village, and the church of which is most delightfully situated, I treated my horse to some oats and myself to a rasher of bacon."

The church that Cobbett knew is Norman and its early 12th century south door is the finest in Surrey. The nave is Norman, but the chancel and tower are 19th century. One enters by the 15th century west porch with a 15th century window above. The 17th century altar rails are particularly appealing and are said to be the best in the County.

Farley Heath

The Romans built a road from Rowhook (just south of Ockley) to Bagshot and on it lies the Romano-British temple at Farley Heath. The temple lies within a 10-acre enclosure which the modern road to Albury from Shamley Green now cuts through. Martin Tupper of Albury (whom we met at the Silent Pool) discovered the site in 1848. He wrote:
"Many a day have I whiled away
Upon hopeful Farley Heath
In the antique soil digging for spoil
Of possible treasure beneath."

Over 1000 coins have been found here and these date from 25 BC to 382 AD, suggesting that the temple was in use in the first century.

What is visible now is an 18ft square inner sanctuary and an outer colonnade marked out on the ground. The ruins were visible above the ground as late as the 17th century before the stones were removed and re-used in local buildings.

There is a collection of the coins and pottery in Guildford Museum, but Tupper's prize find is now in the British Museum. It is a bronze metal strip with the symbol of three Celtic gods – Taranis, Sncellus, and the mother-goddess Nantosvelte.

The temple was, according to Tupper, destroyed by fire in the 5th century.

Albury

Albury Park is open to the public only on certain days. There is, of course, free access to the church inside its grounds. Cobbett was here before and commented: "Take it all together, this is certainly the prettiest garden I ever beheld. There was taste and sound judgement at every step in laying out this place." The original village of Albury was once here, but it was displaced to nearby Weston Street by the previous owner of Albury Manor. Of Tudor origin, the manor has been altered over the years by John and George Evelyn, Sir John Soane and then Pugin, who also restored the church in 1839.

The church is a lovely building of Saxon origin. The nave, north wall and the base of the tower date from this period. The tower itself is Norman and is topped with a distinguished 17th century cupola. One enters via the 16th century brick and timber porch and then through a massive 13th century door, complete with wooden lock and key. The chancel is 13th century and roofless – at least for the time being, for when I was last there a new roof was being built. On the south wall is a mediaeval wall painting of St. Christopher, the patron saint of travellers. The south transept was completed in 1290 and restored by Pugin in vivid and very effective red, blue and gold.

The notable and influential mathematician, William Oughtred, preached here. He was responsible for the introduction of the multiplication sign (x) and, in the early 17th century, many students came to Albury for tuition. He died in 1660 and is buried in the church, as is the 19th century banker and politician, Henry Drummond. Drummond, a previous owner of the manor house, was a founder of the Catholic Apostolic Church and a follower of the early 19th century preacher, Edward Irving. Irving originally preached in Hatton Garden in London, and then started his own church in Regent Square, which became very popular. He was unsuccessfully tried for heresy and eventually came to Albury where he was befriended by Drummond, who was responsible for the construction of the Irvingite Church at a cost of £16,000. Built in a 15th century style, the church stands a few hundred yards north of the exit from Albury Park. One of the beliefs of the Irvingites was that the Second Coming was imminent.

Shere

Shere is Surrey's most famous village and, that being so, is usually choked with traffic, particularly at weekends. It is one of the Tillingbourne villages with a quaint 'olde worlde' atmosphere. The re-fronted White Horse Inn is situated at one side of the village square, and at the other is the immaculately kept church. There is transitional Norman architecture in the lower part of the tower, as evidenced by the windows on the north side.

Shere is renowned for the anchoress, Christine Carpenter. These poor people chose to spend their lives enclosed in cells attached to a church – mostly where sunlight never came. The position of Christine's cell is marked on the north wall of the chancel. Here she was able to receive the sacraments through the quatrefoil and squint. She had to obtain the permission of the Bishop of Winchester to be enclosed and this he gave on 14th August, 1329. Apparently she escaped some three years later, but was promptly returned. The Bishop ordered her to be guarded "with suitable solicitude and competent vigilance" in order that "the said Christine shall not wander from the laudable intention otherwise solemnly undertaken and again run about being torn to pieces by the attacks of the Tempter."

The church is beautifully kept. Inside there are fragments of stained glass in the aisle east window. The south door is Norman and has zig-zag moulding – but is difficult to see. The font has Purbeck marble shafts and there is an early 13th century "Crusader's Chest". These were placed in churches on the order of Innocent III to collect money for the Crusades. At the entrance to the south chapel is displayed a bronze Madonna and Child of 13th century date that was dug up by a dog at nearby Combe Bottom.

Peter Ustinov has associations with Shere. He first appeared on stage here in 1938 with the 'Otherwise Players'.

ROUTE

➠ Leave the M25 at Junction 9 (Leatherhead) and take the A24 for Dorking. Leave Dorking on the A25 for Guildford and 3.2 miles from Dorking (0.5 miles from Wotton Hatch Inn) turn left (signposted Abinger Common, Friday St, Leith Hill). After 0.9 mile turn right and then, after 0.3 miles, turn right at the T-junction for Abinger Church (115459) (A).

➠ **CYCLISTS: route starts here**

➠ Continue for 1 mile, turn right at a T-junction and then left after 0.1 miles onto A25. Continue to Abinger Hammer (096475) (B).

➠ Turn left in Abinger Hammer (signposted Holmbury St.Mary, Forest Green and Ockley). After 2.4 miles turn right for Holmbury St. Mary church (110444) (C).

➠ After 0.1 miles turn right, pass Hollybush Tavern, join a road coming in from the left and continue for 1.4 miles then turn left (signposted Ewhurst, Cranleigh). After 0.9 miles turn right at the Y-junction. Then, after 0.2 miles, turn right (signposted Ewhurst, Cranleigh) and follow road round to the left for 1 mile to Ewhurst church (091405) (D).

➭ Retrace steps for 0.2 miles and continue straight on (signposted Peaslake, Shere, Gomshall). After 1.8 miles turn sharp left (signposted Winterfold), continue for 0.4 miles and turn right. After 1.1 miles turn left. Continue for 1.3 miles and turn right (signposted Shamley Green, Wonersh, Guildford). After 0.4 miles turn right (signposted Shamley Green, Guildford) into Guildford Road. After 0.1 miles turn right at roundabout onto B2128 (signposted Shamley Green) and then, after 0.5 miles, turn right. After 0.7 miles turn right (signposted Albury, Shere) by large pond. Continue for 1 mile to car parking space on the left for Farley Heath (052450) (E).

➭ Maintain direction on road for 2.2 miles where, just before main road, turn sharp right into Albury Park (063478) (F).

➭ Leave Albury Park and turn right and immediate right for 0.3 miles to A25. Turn right, continue for 0.5 miles and turn right for Shere. Continue for 0.4 miles and turn right for Shere (074478) (G).

➭ Leave Shere, return to the A25 and turn right for Dorking, London and M25.

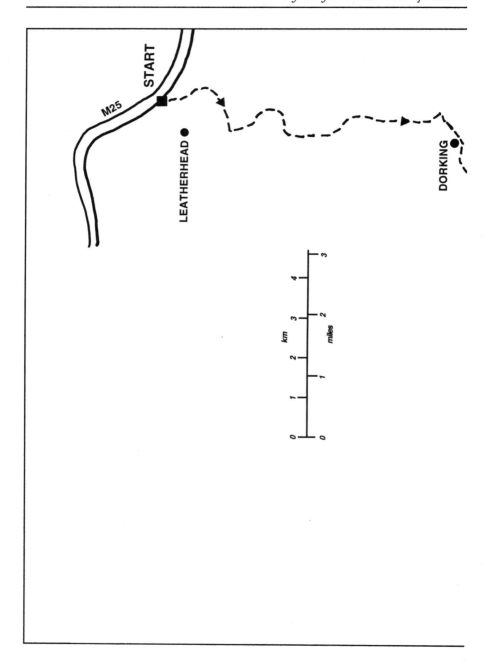

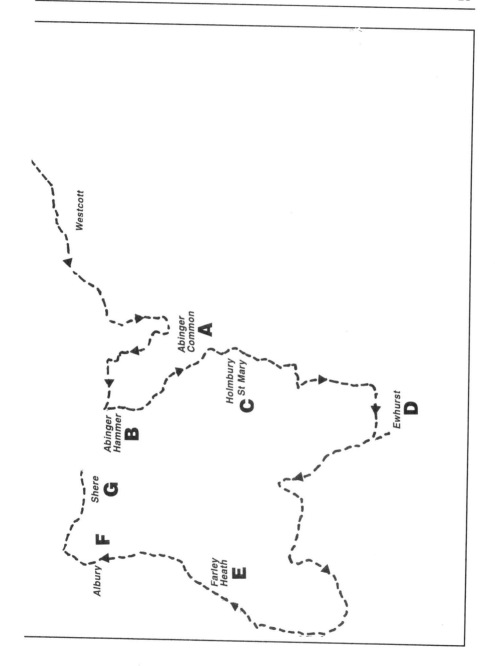

REFRESHMENTS

1. Wotton Hatch Inn – on A25 in Wotton (126475)

2. The Abinger Hatch – opposite Abinger Church (116459)

3. The Abinger Arms – on A25 in Abinger Hammer (096476)

4. The Clockhouse Tea Rooms – on A25 in Abinger Hammer (096475)

5. The Volunteer – in Sutton, between Abinger Hammer and Holmbury St. Mary (107459)

6. The Royal Oak – in Holmbury St.Mary (110444)

8. The Kings Head – in Holmbury St.Mary (112442)

9. The Bulls Head – in Ewhurst (090408)

10. The Windmill Inn – on Pitch Hill north of Ewhurst (080424)

11. Astors Tea Shop – in Shere (073479)

12. The White Horse – in Shere (073478)

13. The Prince of Wales – in Shere (073478)

3: On the bridge, with Nelson

Route: West Humble – Ranmore – Coldharbour –
Ockley – Leith Hill – Friday St – Wotton

Distance: 28 miles/45 km

West Humble

The Burford Bridge Hotel, lying at the foot of Box Hill, used to be
known as the Fox and Hounds, and has had many famous visitors,
including Queen Victoria.

Keats came here in 1817 to "change the scene, change the air and to give
me a spur to wind up my poem." This poem was Endymion, which he
finished on 28th November of that year – the final lines being inspired
by the moonlight on Box Hill. Of the Mole Valley, which is where we
are, Keats wrote "O, thou woulds't joy to live in such a place." Lord
Nelson was another famous guest at the inn. He wrote "A very pretty
place and we are all very happy". He stayed here before Trafalgar with
Lady Hamilton. Robert Louis Stevenson stayed several times between
1878 and 1886.

Three hundred yards along the main road towards Dorking is a bridle
way on the left which leads to the stepping stones across the River Mole.
The crossing here is the same as used by the Canterbury Pilgrims. The
stones, a well-known Surrey beauty spot, were put in place in 1946 at the
expense of the then Home Secretary, Mr. Chuter Ede, and they were
opened by the Prime Minister, Mr. Clement Attlee.

On the way to Ranmore Common the ruined chapel of West Humble is
passed on the left. The chapel is now in the hands of the National Trust,

and their inscription tells us that it was founded at the end of the 12th century for the villagers of West Humble, but desecrated some three centuries later.

Ranmore

Ranmore Common, formerly known as Ashcombe Hill, is some 600 feet high. The Victorian church, known as The Church on the North Downs Way, is a landmark and can be seen from near and far. It was founded by Lord Ashcombe, being built in 1859 by Sir George Gilbert Scott. Lord Ashcombe was the son of Thomas Cubitt, who was responsible for building Belgravia. George Meredith, who lived nearby at Box Hill, knew the church well and referred to it as Cubitt's finger.

The church has a central octagonal tower and, for those interested in Victorian churches, the interior is superb – although the official historic buildings inspector referred to it as having "a certain horrid splendour". It is predominantly marble inside, with marble shafts and naturalistic capitals. The font is maroon and black.

Coldharbour

The name Coldharbour comes from 'cold dwelling' or 'cold shelter'. The village has only a few houses and a pub and is remotely sited, at 700 feet, on the Greensand range of hills.

The Iron Age hill fort, Anstiebury Camp, is at the east of the village, but is difficult to discern or reach. It is covered with trees but is visible looking east from the far end of the village near to the War Memorial. During the Napoleonic wars, the plan was for the women and children of nearby Dorking to take refuge there in case of invasion. Luckily, no invasion came.

Ockley

Ockley lies on the main London to Chichester road. This is the famous Stane Street, built by the Romans in about 60 or 70 AD, to run from London to Chichester. One side of the road is bordered by the enormous village green and to the north is Leith Hill. Being half-way between the Sussex sea ports and London, smuggling was once prevalent in the area.

Indeed, Stane Street at this point was once known as Brandy and Silk Street.

It is very probable that Ockley is the 'Aclea among the Suthridge' mentioned in the Anglo Saxon Chronicle as the site of the bloody battle between the Christian Ethelwolf, King of Wessex, and the heathen invading Danish army. In 851 the Danes sailed up the Thames, after first sacking Canterbury, to meet and defeat Bearthwolf, King of the Mercians, in London. It was their desire to take Winchester, and some say that before the battle at Ockley they camped for the night at Anstiebury Camp. The Danes met their match in Ethelwolf, who won a decisive victory. The historian, F.J.C. Hearnshaw, writes "This was undoubtedly one of the decisive battles of early English history; it saved the country from a premature Danish occupation. Its fame rang throughout Christendom, and encouraged many people in far distant lands to resist the terrible marauders."

The battle went down in legend and one Henry of Huntingdon wrote in 1150: " . . . greater and more obstinate than any that had been heard of in England. You might see there the warriors thick as ears of corn charging upon either hand, and rivers of blood rolling away the heads and limbs of the slain. God gave the fortune of the war to those who believed in Him and ineffable confusion to those who despised Him."

Leith Hill

Leith Hill is a famous Surrey landmark and is the highest point in the southeast of England. With the tower, which stands at its summit, it rises to a height of 1000 feet and so, technically speaking, can be considered a mountain.

With the consent of John Evelyn, the tower was built by Richard Hull in 1766. It was raised in height in 1788 and battlements added in 1864. There is an inscription which says in Latin "That you, traveller, may see the County happy on every side, this tower, visible from afar, was built at the expense of Richard Hull, Esq, of Leith Hill Place, in the reign of King George III, AD 1766, not solely for his own pleasure, but for that of his neighbours and everybody." The tower was closed in the early 19th century because smugglers were using it as a store for their contraband – but it was re-opened in 1863. The view from the top is panoramic and on a clear day the sea can be seen through the Shoreham Gap and from the indicator on the top, the North Downs, Chobham Ridges, Chilterns, Greensand range, South Downs and Ashdown Forest are marked out.

Richard Hull died in 1772 and is buried beneath the tower.

A more recent resident of nearby Leith Hill Place was Ralph Vaughan Williams, the composer. In 1945 he gave the house and 400 acres of land to the National Trust.

Friday Street

A branch of the Tillingbourne runs north from Friday Street and this was dammed in the late 16th century to make the still water we now see. The stream itself joins the east-west flowing Tillingbourne a couple of miles away and flows to meet the Wey near Guildford. Friday Street is thus a mill pond and perhaps not a hammer pond as has been alternatively proposed.

Friday Street

Sad to say, Friday Street is not the birth-place of Stephan Langton, Archbishop of Canterbury at the time of the Magna Carta, as has been suggested in Martin Tupper's unhistorical (as Maxwell Fraser calls it) novel.

Having said all this, the place is wonderfully picturesque and quite justifiably one of Surrey's best-known beauty spots.

Wotton

Wotton was the birth-place and family home of John Evelyn, the notable 17th century diarist. He records in his diary about Wotton – " . . . the distance from London little more than twenty miles, and yet so securely placed, as if it were one hundred". John Evelyn was born here in 1620 and stayed for the first five years of his life. His diary later records that "One Friar taught us at the church porch at Wotton". The church, with its porch, is found at the end of a quiet lane, but unfortunately is frequently locked. The setting is tranquil, with Deer Leap Woods and the White

Wotton Church

Downs as a splendid backdrop. The church has an early Norman tower and members of the Evelyn family are buried in the Evelyn chapel – that is, the north chapel.

Over the arch of the south doorway are eight carved heads, barely three inches in height. Some say that these represent "all sorts and conditions of men" – the theory being that they refer to the Great Interdict imposed by Pope Innocent III in 1213 on England because of King John's defying the Pope at the election of Stephan Langton as Archbishop of

Canterbury. Going from left to right the heads would represent first Cardinal Pandulph (the Papal legate), then a peasant, followed by Queen Isabella. A noble layman comes next, who could be the Patron of the Living, Ralph de Camoys, then there is a priest (the Rector of Wotton) followed by King John. After that there is Pope Innocent III and, finally, Archbishop Stephan Langton.

John Evelyn had a great love of trees and was known as Sylva Evelyn. This probably accounts for his somewhat hostile comments about the local iron industry: "Twere better to purchase all our iron out of America than thus to exhaust our woods at home".

Monument, Wotton Church

ROUTE

➠ Leave the M25 at junction 9 (Leatherhead) and take the A24 towards Dorking. Continue for 4.5 miles to the car park at Burford Bridge (172519) (A).

➠ **FOR CYCLISTS: this is the start of the route**

➠ Rejoin the main A24 and take the first right past the roundabout (signposted West Humble, Box Hill Station). Continue past the Stepping Stones pub to the ruins, in 0.7 miles, of West Humble Chapel (161519) (B).

➠ In 0.4 miles turn left (signposted Ranmore) and continue for 1.4 miles to Ranmore church (146504) (C).

➠ Continue for 0.1 miles and turn left at the T-junction (signposted Dorking). After 1.4 miles turn right at a T-junction in Dorking, and continue for 0.2 miles, where you turn right onto the A25 (signposted Guildford). In 1.5 miles, at the Cricketers pub, turn left, pass Westcott church and take first left into Logmore Lane. In 1.7 miles turn right. Continue for 1.3 miles to Coldharbour and follow road round to the right for 0.4 miles to Coldharbour War Memorial (150439) (D).

➠ Retrace steps and take the first right after 0.4 miles and skirt Anstiebury Camp. Continue for 1.7 miles to main A27 and turn right. Continue to Ockley Common (147400) (E).

➠ Continue for 2.6 miles (from the point where the A27 was joined) and turn right into Cathill Lane. In 0.4 miles turn right into Mole St. In 1.3 miles turn left by joining road coming in from right, and in 0.1 miles turn right (signposted Leith Hill, Friday St, Abinger Common, and Wotton). Maintain direction for 1.2 miles (passing Leith Hill Place), park and walk to the right for Leith Hill (131432) (F).

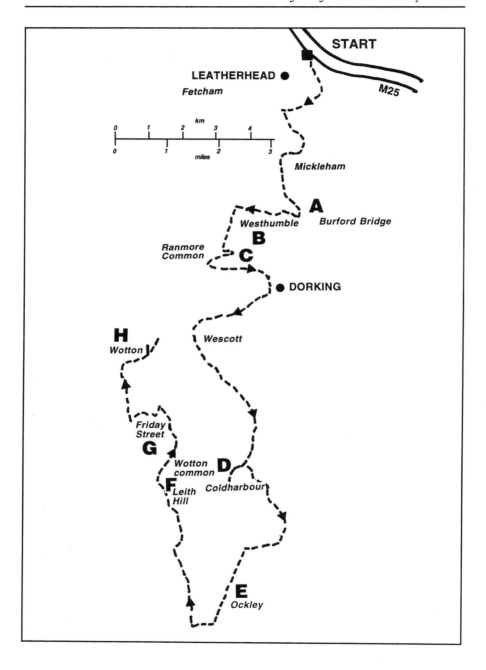

➠ In 0.4 miles turn right (signposted Broadmoor) and in 1.3 miles turn left (signposted Friday Street). Continue for 0.6 miles to car park at Friday Street (126457) (G).

➠ In 0.4 miles turn right and in a further 1.2 miles turn right on to the main A25 (signposted Dorking). In 0.5 miles turn left at the Wotton Hatch Inn for Wotton church (126479) (H).

➠ Retrace steps to the main A25, turn left for Dorking and turn left for the A24 for London and the M25.

REFRESHMENTS

1. The Burford Bridge Hotel – at foot of Box Hill on the A24 (173519)

2. Rykas Good Food Snack Bar – in car park near hotel (173519)

3. The Stepping Stones – by Box Hill/Westhumble railway station (169517)

4. The Pilgrim – in Dorking (162498)

5. The Star – in Dorking (163494)

6. The Crown – on A25 in Westcott (145486)

7. The Prince of Wales – in Westcott (145486)

8. The Cricketers – by church in Westcott (140484)

9. The Plough (highest pub in south east England) – in Coldharbour (153442)

10. The Kings Arms

11. The Red Lion

12. The Cricketers Arms

13. The Old School House – all in Ockley on Stane Street (145400)

14. The Stephan Langton – in Friday Street (127455)

4: Epsom's Capital Views and the Weald-wide vista from Box Hill

Route: Epsom Downs – Mickleham – Box Hill – Brockham – Charlwood – Leigh – Betchworth

Distance: 39 miles/63 km

Epsom Downs

The view from Epsom Downs is magnificent. If the weather is clear, Windsor Castle can be seen over to the left, with the Chiltern Hills beyond. Then, scanning round towards the east, there is first Heathrow Airport, with aircraft taking off and landing. Further round, the two towers of Wembley Stadium can sometimes be seen, and then London itself – with the Post Office tower and Canary Wharf prominent. On a really clear day, Alexander Palace can be located with the aid of binoculars. Binoculars also help to identify individual buildings in London.

The chalk downs fall away to the north to Epsom town, once called Ebbe's home – that is, the home of Princess Ebbe, a 5th century Saxon princess. Epsom's heyday was in the 17th century, for in 1618 the well was discovered which yielded the famous Epsom salts (magnesium sulphate). The discovery is said to have been made by cattle who refused to drink the water gushing from a spring. There were many famous visitors to the well, including Charles II and Nell Gwynne. Samuel Pepys was a frequent visitor to Epsom and his diary of 14th July, 1667, tells us

Wooden graveboard, Mickleham Church

that he drank four pints of the nauseous liquid. Epsom's popularity declined in the early 18th century, when the wells dried up, and the rise of nearby Tunbridge Wells did nothing to help.

A new lease of life was given to the town, however, by the 12th Earl of Derby, whose home – The Oaks – was nearby, beyond Banstead Downs. It was during a party there that he founded two horse races, the first in 1779 named after his house "The Oaks" and then, in 1780, The Derby.

Prime Minister between 1894 and 1895, Lord Roseberry lived at Epsom and he describes the coming of The Derby and The Oaks thus: "Though the waters failed us, a miracle yet remained to be wrought on behalf of Epsom. In the last quarter of the 18th century, a roistering party at a neighbouring country house founded two races, in two successive years: one for three-year-old colts and fillies, and the other for three-year-old fillies, and named them gratefully after their host and his house – the Derby and the Oaks. Seldom has a carouse had a permanent effect. Up to that time, Epsom had enjoyed little more than the ordinary races of a market town."

The whole scene of the rolling downs is dominated by the Epsom grandstand. Built in 1927, it was the first stand of this type to be constructed with reinforced concrete. A new stand and conference suite were completed in 1992. There have been races on these Downs since Henry VIII's day. The most famous of all horses was Eclipse – born in 1764 during the eclipse of that time and never beaten in any race.

Mickleham

Mickleham is approached from Headley through glorious downland scenery, known locally as 'Little Switzerland'. At the T-junction the church of St Michael is to the right. It is Norman but has been heavily restored. The west tower and west doorway are original, but the aisles date from Victorian times. The pulpit dates from 1600 and is Belgian in origin. Outside, near the lychgate to the south, is a perfectly preserved wooden graveboard. It is to one John Walker, who died in 1813. The inscription reads:

Farewell all my friends so kind
I hope in Heaven my soul you'll find

Also in the churchyard, east of the church and to the right of a path running north-south, is the grave of Douglas Graham Gilmour. He was one of the pioneers of flight and his grave is marked by a miniature metal aeroplane. Gilmour first flew in Paris in 1909 and later bought a Bleriot monoplane, known as the Big Bat. By nature he was daring to the point of recklessness – flying over Hampton Court at a height of 200 feet and then at Henley Regatta with wheels touching the River Thames. He eventually crashed fatally in Richmond Park at the age of 26.

A walk down the road to the north of the church leads to the splendid by-pass and then the River Mole. But first, on the right, there is the imposing Old House, dated 1636, with Dutch gables and Ionic pilasters to its gate.

The Mole at Mickleham has a tendency to dry up in hot summers, but the waters flow underground in the chalk and then emerge downstream. They are known as the swallows of the Mole, and the phenomenon has attracted interest for many years. For instance, in 1700 Celia Fiennes wrote that the Mole " . . . runs twiyning itself about and is called the Swallow, and just about Dorken and Leatherhead it sinkes away in many places which they call swallow holes; this must be some quick sand, but the report of it is it sinkes here and runnes underground a mile or two and rises about Molesey and runnes again. Camden does credit this and repeats a tryal once made of forcing a duck into one of these falls which came out at the other side by Molesey with its feathers allmost all rubbed off". It is said that the swallows are capable of taking in 30 million gallons of water each day.

Further towards Dorking from the church is Juniper Hall, with its impressive *porte-cochere*. It is now a field study centre, but in the late 18th century it was home to a group of refugees from the French Revolution. It was here that the novelist Fanny Burney met her husband, as the inscription on the gate tells us: "This house gave shelter in 1792 to a group of progressive French aristocrats who had fled to England to escape the worst excesses of the French Revolution. The group included Alexandre d'Arblay and Talleyrand. It was here that Fanny Burney, the novelist, as a visitor to her sister Susanne Phillips of Mickleham, met Alexandre d'Arblay, to whom she was subsequently married at Mickleham church".

Also married at Mickelham church was the Victorian poet and novelist George Meredith in 1864. His house was Flint Cottage, which is on the left as the zigzag of Box Hill is ascended. He wrote of his house: "Anything grander than the days and nights in my porch you will not find away from the Alps".

Box Hill

The road climbs up through hairpin bends to Box Hill – so called because of the box trees (a very heavy wood) that grow here. The view over the Weald from the 650 ft viewpoint is spectacular and one of the grandest in the southeast of England.

Now in the hands of the National Trust, there is a shop belonging to this organisation near the tea rooms and between this and the summit is Swiss Cottage – once belonging to John Logie Baird, the inventor of television, who lived here between 1929 and 1932.

There are many literary associations with the area, for instance Box Hill was the picnic spot in Jane Austen's 'Emma'.

A curious monument is found near to the footpath that leads west to Dorking. It is to Peter Labelliere. He was buried head down – believing that the world was upside down and therefore to be buried in this way was entirely appropriate.

John Evelyn wrote in his diary in 1665 describing a visit to Box Hill thus: "I went to Box Hill to see those same natural boxes. Here are such goodly walkes and hills, shaded with yew and box, as to render the place extremely agreeable, it seeming from these evergreens to be summer all the winter".

Brockham

They no longer play cricket on the village green at Brockham, but the green once made a perfect setting for our summer game – indeed W.G. Grace has played here.

The name Brockham is taken from the badgers that one finds hereabouts and the village green makes for a perfect rural scene, with church, two pubs and rows of cottages surrounding it.

There is a wonderful view to the north to the escarpment of the Downs and the place is altogether splendid. Brockham's admirers are not universal, however, for one Captain Morris, a punchmaker at a London club in the Regency, who died at Brockham, aged 93, writes:

"In town let me live, then, in town let me die,
For in truth I can't relish the country, not I.
If one must have a villa in summer to dwell,
O give me the sweet shady side of Pall Mall."

Charlwood

Charlwood takes its name from the wood of churl – churls being free people in the Saxon era. Around the church there are tile-hung cottages and the Half Moon pub. The church is approached along a long stone path with a meadow to the left and the roar of aeroplanes above from nearby Gatwick. One enters through the 15th century south porch with sundial, dated 1791, above. This commemorates the church wardens of the day.

The church was originally Norman, as evidenced by the window in the north side of the nave and the crossing tower. Later, in the 13th century, a south aisle and then, in the 15th century, a south chapel were added and these now serve as nave and chancel in today's church.

People visit the church to see the wall paintings on the south wall of the nave. These were discovered in 1858 and date from the 14th century. The one on the left tells the story of St Margaret of Antioch. Margaret's father was a pagan priest, but she was brought up as a Christian by her nurse. When she grew up she became a shepherdess and, while tending her sheep, she attracted the interest of Olibrius, the governor of Antioch. Because Olibrius was a pagan she refused to marry him and for this was promptly thrown in jail by the angry Olibrius.

The element of fantasy now enters the story – she was first swallowed whole by a dragon, but escaped after the intervention of Providence, only to be beheaded on Olibrius' orders. Her soul, depicted as a dove, then ascended to heaven.The upper tier of the painting shows Olibrius out hunting on horseback. The middle tier shows, from left to right, Margaret being beaten with rods, then in prison, then being swallowed by the dragon, then escaping. The lower tier shows a prison scene, Margaret being beheaded, and then ascending to Heaven.

The painting to the west shows, up above, scenes from the life of St Nicholas and, below, the Three Living and the Three Dead (three kings on horseback encountering three skeletons).

Between nave and chancel there is an intricate late perpendicular screen, full of life. It has decorative painted cresting above, with vine trail and winged dragons. Angels hold the monogram IHS and there is a crowned letter M. Also included are the initials RS. These refer to Richard Sanders, who died in 1480.

The Sanders were a well-known family and lived at nearby Charlwood Place, just north of the village. Here, in 1530, was born Nicholas Sanders. He was a fervent Roman Catholic and in the Elizabethan era travelled to Rome and then Madrid. Here, he conspired against Elizabeth by encouraging Philip of Spain to mount an invasion of England from Ireland. His aim was to install Mary Queen of Scots on the English throne, and in support of this he promised the help of 5000 men. All came to nothing and he eventually died in Ireland in exile in 1581.

Leigh

Leigh has everything that people associate with a village. It has a village green surrounded by pub, school, half-timbered houses and a church. To the north is the weatherboarded pub called the Plough. There is a Victorian school and, to the south, the long range of the 15th century Priests House, half-timbered and with a Horsham slate roof. The church of St Bartholomew is originally 15th century but was restored in 1890. It has a pretty, lean-to Victorian porch at its west end.

To the north is the Gothic Leigh Place – originally 17th century but rebuilt in distinctive style in 1810.

Leigh Place, Leigh

Betchworth

There is obviously a very active local history society at Betchworth, for in the church can be found an extensive series of leaflets and booklets describing the village both past and present. The oldest item in the church is the fragment of Saxon capital – eight circular roll mouldings – to be found reset in the west side of the south window of the tower. Also under the tower is the old parish chest – shaped from the solid trunk of an oak tree and dating back to mediaeval times.

On a pillar on the south side of the nave is the memorial to Sir Benjamin Brodie, Surgeon to the Queen (Victoria) and President of the Royal Society. Brodie lived from 1783 to 1862 and was also President of the Royal College of Surgeons and is eponymously remembered as the describer of Brodie's abscess of bone. We are told that Isambard Brunel, the famous engineer, was one of his patients. Brunel was once unfortunate enough to swallow half a sovereign, which Brodie rescued by placing his patient head down in a revolving frame.

The road from the church leads to the main street in which can be found Old House, described by Pevsner as 18th century and as stark as a warehouse – but according to the local historians, much older. Then, further on is the Dolphin pub, 17th century with a mansard roof. East from the Dolphin and along the lane to the south is More Place, an exquisite building dating from the 15th century.

ROUTE

➤ Leave the M25 at junction 9 (Leatherhead) and proceed to Epsom on the A24. At the far end of Epsom High Street (the east end) take the B284 (signposted to Epsom Downs). In 0.4 miles carry straight on to the B284 (signposted Burgh Heath) and in 1.2 miles turn right at roundabout (last exit, signposted Ashtead). Continue for 0.4 miles to the car park on the right on Epsom Downs (220587) (A).

➤ **FOR CYCLISTS: this is the start of the route**

➤ Continue to roundabout and maintain direction. Pass the grand-stand and turn first left into Langley Vale Road. Continue for 1.3 miles and turn left at a T-junction (signposted Headley). After 0.3 miles keep right at the Y-junction and continue for 2.0 miles, where you turn right (signposted Dorking, Leatherhead). In 0.5 miles turn left (signposted Mickleham, Dorking). Continue for 2.2 miles through 'Little Switzerland' and at the T-junction turn right. After 0.5 miles park at Mickleham church (171535) (B).

➤ Retrace steps for 0.5 miles, for Juniper Hall (173527) (C).

➤ Continue for 0.1 miles and turn left (signposted Box Hill). Pass Flint Cottage on the left and continue for 1.6 miles to the car park on the summit of Box Hill (179513) (D).

➤ Continue for 2.5 miles and turn right (signposted Tadworth, Reigate), and in 0.1 miles turn right again (signposted Dorking, Reigate, Betchworth). After 1.4 miles carry straight on at round-about, crossing the A25 (signposted Betchworth, Leigh, Charlwood). After 0.2 miles turn right (signposted Brockham). In 0.2 miles turn left (signposted Brockham, Newdigate). In 0.7 miles, turn left into Brockham Lane (signposted Brockham, Newdigate). Continue for 0.2 miles to Brockham (197495) (E).

➠ Maintain direction for 2.8 miles and then turn right at a T-junction (signposted Newdigate). In 1.2 miles turn left (signposted Charlwood, Horley), and in a further 0.3 miles turn left (signposted Charlwood, Horley). In 2.6 miles turn right at the T-junction (signposted Charlwood, Horley). Ignoring the first right turn, turn sharp right after 0.2 miles (opposite post office) for Charlwood church (241411) (F).

➠ Continue round and turn left at main road, continue straight ahead (signposted Leigh) and after 0.3 miles pass Charlwood Place on the right. Continue for 3.9 miles, and turn right at the Plough Inn at Leigh (225469) (G).

➠ In 0.2 miles pass Leigh Place on the right and at a T-junction turn left (signposted Newdigate, Dorking). In 0.3 miles turn right (signposted Brockham, Dorking, Newdigate) and then first right at Seven Stars Inn (signposted Betchworth). In 1.9 miles turn left for Betchworth church (211497) (H).

➠ Retrace steps, turn right into main road and then left into Wonham Lane at Dolphin Inn. In 0.2 miles pass More Place on right. Continue to a T-junction, turn left and continue to the A25 where you turn right for Reigate, then left on to the A217 for London and the M25.

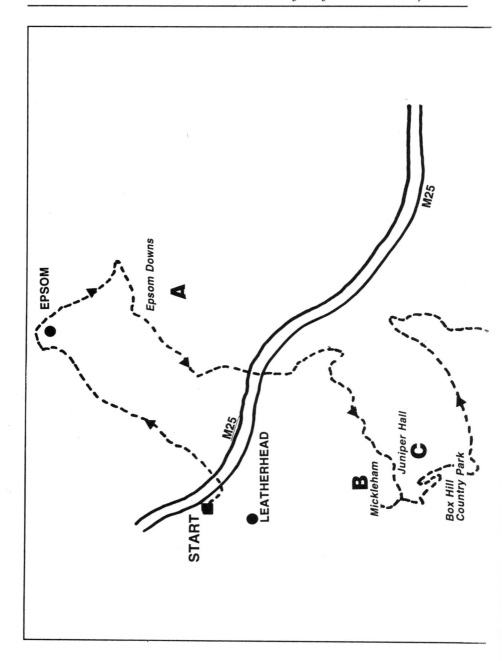

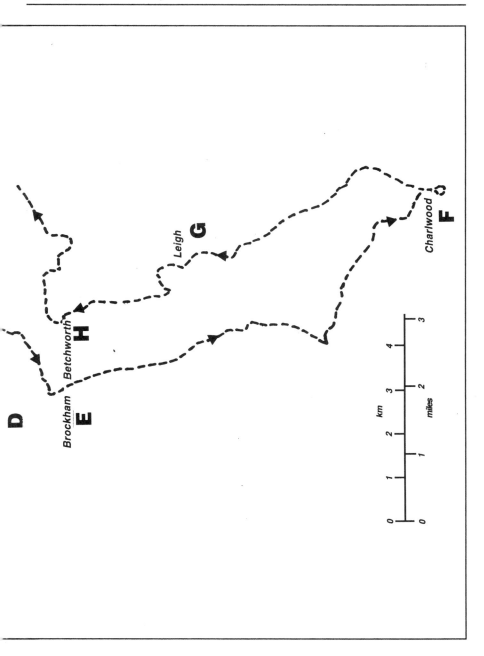

REFRESHMENTS

1. The Derby Arms – opposite Epsom Grandstand (217587)

2. The Rubbing House – adjacent to Epsom Grandstand (215585)

3. The Cock Inn – in Headley village between Epsom Downs and Mickleham (204546)

4. The Running Horses – in Mickleham opposite the church (170534)

5. The Old Fort(National Trust Shop) – on Box Hill (178513)

6. The Hand in Hand – just past Box Hill village (203520)

7. The Royal Oak.

8. The Dukes Head – both on Brockham village green (197496)

9. The Spotted Cow – south of Brockham village (201484)

10. The Half Moon – in Charlwood by the church (242412)

11. The Fox Revived – between Charlwood and Leigh (239436)

12. The Plough – in Leigh village (224469)

13. The Seven Stars – between Leigh and Betchworth (218472)

14. The Dolphin – in Betchworth village (212497)

5: A Mediaeval Painting – and a Vile and Rotten Borough

Route: Coulsdon – Chaldon – Bletchingley – Outwood – Godstone

Distance: 20 miles/32 km

Coulsdon

High up on the downs above Coulsdon are Farthing Downs – so called because many Roman coins, including farthings, have been discovered here.

The Saxons inhabited these parts and it is speculated that they came here by sailing up the River Wandle, which flows into the Thames at present-day Wandsworth, and which rises in nearby Croydon. Fourteen ancient barrows have been identified and dated as 6th or 7th century. A Mr. John Wickham Flower opened them in 1872 and found in one the remains of a body with a drinking cup of wood with bronze bands and decorated with the head of a snake. In another he found the intact remains of a mighty warrior with sword.

Mr. Flower reasoned that because Coulsdon derives from *Cuthredesdune*, the warrior could well be the Anglo-Saxon prince Cuthred, King of Wessex, who was baptised at Dorchester in 639.

Chaldon

Set high on the north Downs, in its tranquil setting, is the church of St
Peter and St Paul, Chaldon. Inside is one of the most famous wall
paintings in the country. The painting was discovered in 1870 and is of
12th century date. It measures 17ft by 11ft and covers the church's west
wall. It is known as the Ladder of Salvation and comprises two
compartments – the upper representing Purgatory and the lower Hell.
Joining the two is the ladder of salvation, where souls are seen climbing
to escape from Hell to Heaven, where Christ is seen in a cloud. In the
left compartment of Hell are two devils and a cauldron, and in the right
compartment are two further devils holding the bridge of spikes
carrying craftsmen trying, in vain, to carry on their trades but being
prevented from doing so because the blacksmiths have no anvil, the
potter no wheel, and so on. Also in the right compartment of Hell is a
coiled serpent representing the beginning of life in the Tree of
Knowledge.

In the upper Purgatorial level, angels help souls off the ladder. On the
left the Archangel Michael weighs souls, while Satan tries to gain an
unfair advantage by depressing the scales to gain more victims. The
right panel shows a representation of the Harrowing of Hell.

The seven deadly sins are shown in the lower panel. Pevsner describes
them (from left to right): Sloth – three souls trying to walk with a beast
below instead of firm ground; Gluttony – a pilgrim discarding his coat
for a bottle; Pride – a woman lifting her arm grasped by a beast; Anger –
two fighting figures; Lust – a couple embracing with a devil in
attendance; Avarice – a figure with money bags round his neck and
waist; and Envy – a figure attracting another with a devil stopping him.

The church itself has a tower with shingled spire of 1843, but is mainly
of the 12th to 13th century. The pulpit is unusual in that it is from the
Cromwellian period and dated 1657.

Bletchingley

Bletchingley

The drive from Chaldon to Bletchingley passes four houses of historic or architectural interest. First, on the left and in its own grounds is Pendell Court, built in 1624 and now a school. Then, on the right, is Pendell House. This is ascribed to Richard Glyd, but its construction was influenced by Inigo Jones.

Further round is the 15th century Brewer Street farmhouse. This lovely house has a hipped Horsham slate roof and two gables. It is on the left of the lane.

Brewer Street, Bletchingley

Place Farm, on the left, has remains of the long-since demolished Bletchingley Place. This large mansion was built in 1517 by the Duke of Buckingham and was occupied by Anne of Cleves after her divorce from Henry VIII. All that remains now is the gatehouse, and this can be clearly seen at the entrance to Place Farm.

Bletchingley is a pleasant place, now relatively free of traffic since the building of the M25. The church was restored in 1910 and is mainly perpendicular with a Norman west tower. Its most remarkable feature is the exuberant monument to Sir Robert Clayton. Clayton, who was Lord Mayor of London between 1679 and 1680, commissioned Robert Crutcher to erect the monument in honour of his wife. This was in 1707, still in the lifetime of Sir Robert. The monument is now recognised as one of the best 18th century monuments in the country, but this has not always been so, for in 1876 Louis Jennings wrote of it: "The figures, the angels, the inscription, everything about it is like a fearful nightmare".

Near to the Clayton monument, a quatrefoil in the south wall of the south chapel is positioned on the site of an anchorite cell once occupied in the 13th century by one Brother Roger, a hermit who is said to have been an early Franciscan.

Bletchingley has associations with the people of the island of Tristan-da-Cunha. A model sailing boat in the church, a gift of the people of Tristan-da-Cunha, commemorates the time in 1961 when, after a volcano erupted on their island, the islanders were evacuated to Bletchingley.

On the south side of the High Altar is the monument to Sir Thomas Cawarden. He was Master of the Revels to four sovereigns and his changing religious principles can be seen as a reaction to the times. He was an enthusiastic reformer under Edward VI, but became a Catholic in Mary Tudor's reign. He eventually died in the Tower of London when Elizabeth I was queen.

West of the church is the attractive Church Row, and this leads eventually to the site of the castle. Only a mound remains today of the castle of Richard de Tonebridge, which was demolished in 1264 by Prince Edward.

Over the road from the church is the Tudor White Hart Inn, and it was from here that elections were held for the two members that Bletchingley sent to parliament. That is, before the Reform Bill of 1832, for Bletchingley was, in the words of Cobbett "a vile Rotten borough". One of its members was Lord Palmerston, and in the 1830s the total number of voters numbered 12 – but it must be said in Palmerston's defence that he was a supporter of the Reform Bill.

In Stuart times, the rector of Bletchingley, Dr Nathaniel Harris (he is buried in the north aisle of the church) favoured a Mr. Lovell as member of parliament, and he did his best to ensure his return by preaching sermons specifically directed against those who would not give him their vote – referring to his opponents as lying knaves. In due course Mr. Lovell was successful in getting to parliament, but a petition against Harris, accusing him of bribery, forced him to kneel at the bar of the House of Commons, confess his fault and pray for pardon. This he had to do, once more, the following Sunday in church at Bletchingley.

Outwood

Legend tells us that the people of the small hamlet of Outwood were able to see the bright red glow in the sky as London burned during the great fire of 1666. This was just one year after the post mill, still standing and also used as a small zoo and rural museum, was first built.

There were once two mills here next to one another. They were known as the kitten and the cat. The older of the two is the one we see today, the younger one having fallen down during gales in 1960. It was originally built after a feud between the two brothers who owned the original mill. Its purpose was to act as a rival.

Outwood Mill

Godstone

There was originally a Saxon settlement at what is now Godstone. It was known as Wolcherstede, but no trace now remains. The church was extensively restored by the famous Victorian architect, Sir Giles Gilbert Scott, whose house in the 1870s was at Rooksnest – a little way to the north and now a school. It was Scott who designed the St Mary's almshouses for Mrs. Mabel Hunt immediately south of the church. These Tudor Gothic buildings were put up in 1872 and form an attractive group of eight houses and chapel. They were modernised in 1973.

St Mary's Almhouses

Godstone lies on the intersection of the A25 and the Roman road from London to Lewes. The name is probably taken from Goda's town – Goda being the sister of Edward the Confessor. William Cobbett was very familiar with Godstone and described it as "a beautiful village, chiefly of one street, with a fine large green before it, and with a pond in the green".

This fine large green and pond are still there today and, as with all fine village greens, has cricket in the summer. In 1912 the famous Jack Hobbs played here for Surrey against a team from Godstone. He was fortunate not to be given out after just three balls, but the umpire ruled 'not out'. Later, in the local hostelry, the decision was challenged by the Godstone side, to which the umpire responded: "Yes, he was out, clean as a whistle, but everyone was here to see Hobbs batting". In the end, Hobbs and his partner had a stand of 172 and Surrey finally declared at 421 for 4. The umpire's decision cost the Godstone team dearly – they were all out for 54.

Opposite the village green is the 16th century White Hart Hotel – once called the Clayton Arms after Sir Robert Clayton, whom we met in Bletchingley. Many famous visitors have stayed at this welcoming inn, including Queen Victoria and, of course, William Cobbett in his Rural Rides. The Czar of Russia was accommodated here in 1815 when he attended a prize fight at nearby Blindley Heath.

In the 16th century, Godstone had a thriving gunpowder industry run by the Evelyn brothers.

ROUTE

⇒ Approach Coulsdon either from Croydon and Purley on the A23, or from the M25 via the M23 intersection. Proceed south from Smitham station and after 0.3 miles turn left on to the B2030 (Marlpit Lane, signposted Old Coulsdon). After passing beneath two railway bridges, take the second right into Downs Road and continue for 1.1 miles for parking place on Farthing Down (301572) (A).

⇒ **FOR CYCLISTS: this is the start of the route**

⇒ Continue ahead for 1.1 miles and turn right for Chaldon church (308557) (B).

⇒ Continue, and after 0.5 miles carry straight on at crossroad (Hill Top Lane). After 1.5 miles turn left at the T-junction (signposted Nutfield and Bletchingley). Pass Pendell Court on the left and Pendell House (315518) (C) on the right and in 1.1 miles turn left (signposted Caterham). Brewer Street farm (325519) (D) is on the left after 0.6 miles. Take the first right (signposted Godstone and Bletchingley), pass Place Farm (327521) (E) on the left and continue for 1 mile to Bletchingley (327507) (F) (cars can be parked to the right in the main street, A25).

⇒ From Bletchingley church continue south (i.e. cross A25) for 3.5 miles, where just past the Bell Inn turn left (signposted Horne, Blindley Heath) for Outwood Windmill (327455) (G).

⇒ Continue for 1.3 miles and turn left (signposted Blindley Heath and Godstone). Maintain direction for 2.0 miles to the A22 and turn left (signposted Godstone and Caterham). After 0.2 miles turn left into Tilburstow Hill Road. After 2.2 miles turn right, and then right again at a T-junction (A22). Take first left into Church Lane for,after 0.4 miles, Godstone church (357515) (H).

⇒ Continue for 0.3 miles and turn left at the T-junction (A25, signposted Godstone). After 0.5 miles turn left at roundabout and continue on the A22 for Godstone village centre (350515) (I).

⇒ Retrace steps on the A22 for the M25 and London.

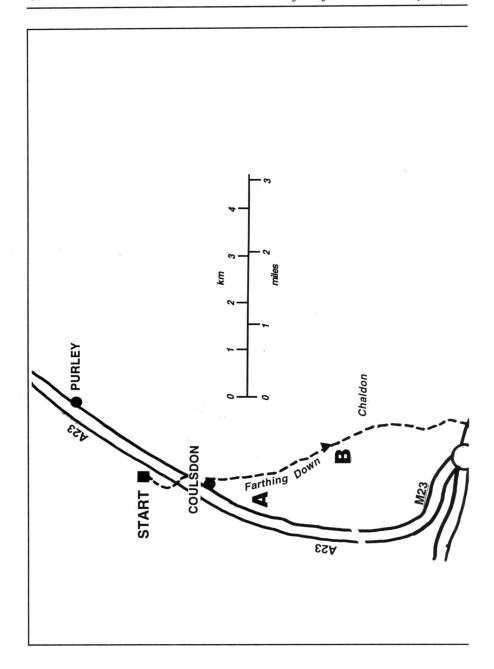

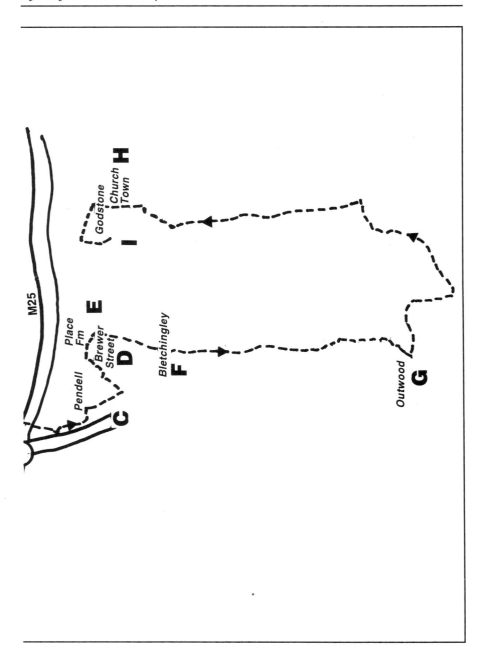

REFRESHMENTS

1. The Welcome Tea Rooms

2. Downlands Restaurant – both on Farthing Downs (302572)

3. The Whyte Hart

4. The Prince Albert – both in Bletchingley (327507)

5. The Bell Inn – just before entering Outwood village (328456)

6. The Jolly Farmer – between Outwood and the A22 (347451)

7. The Fox and Hounds – just before Tilburstow Hill south of Godstone (355494)

8. The White Hart

9. The Cauldron

10. The Bell Inn

11. The Godstone Hotel

12. The Old Forge

13. The Hare and Hounds – all in Godstone (350515)

6: A Yorkshire Composer and the Cobham Family Monuments

Route: Farleigh – Limpsfield – Crowhurst – Lingfield – Squerryes Court

Distance: 32 miles/51 km

Farleigh Church

Farleigh

J Charles Cox, in his *Rambles in Surrey* published in 1910, describes Farleigh as "one of the least attractive of the rural parishes of the county". One wonders what has happened to the county since then, for it is now surely one of the more attractive. It is a tiny and remote parish, the smallest in Surrey, and yet is only a few miles south of suburban London.

There is a diminutive Norman church built by Robert de Watville with a Norman west door. Norman also are the windows of the nave. The east window of the chancel, which was extended in 1250, contains two Early English lancets.

In the Middle Ages, Farleigh was a centre for the manufacture of oak shingles (roofing tiles) and also iron nails.

Limpsfield

Limpsfield is a place of pilgrimage for music lovers, for in its churchyard

is buried the composer Frederick Delius. The church itself is a large building with a sturdy tower and pyramidal roof built around 1180. Inside there are early English lancets and in the east wall of the chancel are the remains of a recess used formerly as an oven for baking the communion bread.

To the north of the churchyard, by a yew tree, is the grave of the composer, Frederick Delius. He was born in Yorkshire, at Bradford, but left there when he was 20. His travels took him first to Florida and then to Germany to study, but the greater part of his life was spent in France, and it was here that he died (and was also buried) at Grez-sur-Loing in 1934. It had always been his wish to be buried in an English churchyard, and so it was that his body was brought back here by his wife one year later. The funeral at Limpsfield was a majestic affair and Sir Thomas Beecham, the famous conductor, gave an oration by torchlight. Buried in the adjacent grave is the cellist, Beatrice Harrison, who was also involved in Delius's return to England.

Also buried here is Harriet Kennard, a saintly lady. She was in her eighties when the railway nearby was being built by French labourers. Many of them fell ill with cholera and the disease reached epidemic proportions. Harriet Kennard fearlessly nursed them until she caught the disease herself.

Although on a small scale, there are many beautifully maintained buildings in the High Street, which has been designated a conservation area, and a walk to view them is well worthwhile. Starting to the north, and just around the corner, is Old Court Cottage. After the Norman Conquest, Limpsfield was given to the abbey at Battle and there are parts of this house which date from those times. Then, opposite the church, is the Rectory, a late 17th century brick house. Further up, at the corner of Detillens Lane, is a charming group of 16th to 18th century tile-hung and timber-framed cottages, and then Detillens, a 15th century hall house with an 18th century front. In the summer the house is occasionally open to the public. On the other side of the road is Old Court House, now divided into three but once a 15th century hall house, and then again on the west side is the lovely grouping of Rosewell and Jessamine Cottages, ending with Chapel Cottage. Finally, on the right at the top of the High Street on the corner of the A25, is The Bower, another splendid 17th century house.

Detillens Lane, Limpsfield

It is said that Major Baden-Powell and Colonel Cody – better known as Buffalo Bill, flew man-lifting kites on nearby Limpsfield Common.

Crowhurst

Set in the heart of the Weald, Crowhurst is peaceful and free from all development. Its Early English church stands on high ground and is remarkable for two unique fea-
tures. First, there is the enorm-
ous hollow yew tree, standing supported by crutches and ele-
ven yards in circumference in the churchyard. It has a pad-
locked door (the tree, that is!) and is said once to have con-
tained a bench for twelve people to sit around a table. Also, a cannon ball is claimed to have been discovered within it – probably from a skirmish during the Civil War between the Par-
liamentary forces and the family who lived at Mansion House Farm, who were fervent loyal-
ists. The tree is said to be fifteen hundred years old, and such is its fame that Queen Victoria and the Prince Consort came to view it, riding all the way from Windsor.

The yew tree, Crowhurst

Within the chancel of the church there is a cast iron monument to Anne Foster dated 1591, reminding us once more that the Weald in mediaeval times was a centre for the iron industry. The slab shows a figure in a shroud with panels depicting her five daughters and two sons. Replicas of the slab have been used as firebacks!

Opposite the church is Mansion House Farm, of mediaeval origin but now with a 17th century front. The Angell family once lived here. John Angell was the last survivor of this family. He died in 1784 and in his will he decreed that all of his property should be left to "male heirs, if any there be, of William Angell the first purchaser of Crowhurst in the time of King James". Many people came forward, but none could provide adequate proof.

Further south is Crowhurst Place, a yeoman's house of 1425, but very much restored in 1918. It is difficult to see from the road. Henry VIII was a caller here on his way to Hever to court Anne Boleyn.

Mansion House Farm, Crowhurst

Lingfield

Lingfield is best known for its racecourse. Renowned also is the cross and cage which stands in the village centre. This is known as St Peter's Cross. The inscription upon it tells us: "This cross was built circa 1473 to designate the boundaries of Puttenden and Bileshurst Manors. The cage for the detention of petty offenders added in 1773 was last used in 1882 to detain poachers". The cage was formerly used as a museum but is now empty.

The most charming part of Lingfield is the small roadway leading to the church. On the right is the Star Inn, reminding us that a few miles to the east was Sterborough Castle – now demolished, but formerly the home of the Cobham family. On the left is the 16th century tile-hung and timber-framed Old Town Stores and Pollard Cottage, a 15th century house with shop front used as a butcher's shop until filled in.

It was Reginald, third Lord Cobham of Sterborough, who rebuilt the church in 1431, now dedicated to St Peter and St Paul. He also founded a college in 1432 for a Provost, six chaplains, four clerks of the Carthusian Order and thirteen poor people. This was sited at the west of the church, where now stands a fine house built around 1700 called The College. It is brick with mullioned and transomed windows, tile-hung and has a fine Horsham slate roof.

The tower of the church is 14th century but the remainder is the noble perpendicular building of 1431. Its interior is on a grand scale, light and spacious. There are 15th century screens between the chancel and chapels and impressive misericords beneath the seats in the choir.

The church is best known for its monuments to the Cobham family. Starting in the Lady Chapel (the North Chapel) there is the tomb of Reginald, first Baron Cobham of Sterborough. It is of Caen stone, with battlements and the effigy in armour. The first Baron Cobham was born in 1295. He fought in France in the 14th century and was one of the bodyguards of the Black Prince at the Battle of Crecy in 1346. Later in 1356 he was at Poitiers where he had custody of the King of France. He died of plague in 1361.

Also in the Lady Chapel, on its north side, is the tomb, with Purbeck marble top and brass figure, of the second Lord Cobham. He was one of the commissioners ruling during the minority of Richard II in 1387. Later, however, in 1397 he was exiled by Richard where he met, in Brittany, Henry Bolingbroke, with whom he returned to England to overthrow Richard. Bolingbroke, as Shakespeare tells us in Henry IV, Act II, Scene I, later became Henry IV. The second Lord Cobham married his cousin for which he had to secure dispensation from the Pope. His penance was severe. There was to be: no meat for four years; no wine on Wednesdays; on the six fast days they should eat fish, which was disagreeable to them; they had to feed four poor persons daily and wait upon them themselves. The poor persons were to have bread and meat or fish with half a flagon of ale and were to have new tunics and new russet hoods each year. I wonder whether they kept to this or, for that matter, did they even attempt it?

In the chancel there is the tomb to the founder of the college and the builder of the church, Sir Reginald, third Lord Cobham of Sterborough, and his second wife, Anne Bardolph – both figures in alabaster. Sir Reginald was born in 1382 and fought at Agincourt in 1415. His daughter, Eleanor, married the youngest son of Henry IV, Humphrey, Duke of Gloucester. By 1435 he was the sole remaining son of Henry IV – all the others having died – and accordingly heir-presumptive to the throne. Fate was unkind to Eleanor, however, for in 1441 she was accused of using "sorcery and enchantment" to induce the death of the then-childless Henry VI. She was banished to the Isle of Man, where she spent the rest of her life.

Squerryes Court

Squerryes Court, sited near to the source of the River Darent, is a distinguished red brick house built in 1681 in the Queen Anne style. To the front is a lake and at the rear are gardens laid out when the house was built. It is not the first house on this site. During the reign of Henry III a family known as de Squerie lived here. In the following centuries the old house changed hands many times. The notable diarist, John Evelyn, was a visitor in 1658 and wrote "A pretty, finely wooded, well watered seate, the stables good, the house old, but convenient." In 1681 Sir Nicholas Crisp, the then owner, demolished the old house and built the one we now see.

In 1731 the house came into the possession of the Warde family and it has remained in their hands ever since. The house has associations with James Wolfe (see Westerham) who was a friend of George Warde, for when he was fourteen Wolfe received his first commission at Squerryes. The event is commemorated by the cenotaph in the garden. Letters and commissions of Wolfe are still held by the Warde family. There are many fine pictures and furniture in the house, which is open to the public.

ROUTE

➠ Approach Purley either south from Croydon (A23) or north from the M25 via the M23 intersection. Leave Purley on the A22 (signposted Eastbourne) and after 0.4 miles from main crossroads bear left on to the A2022 (signposted Selsdon, Sanderstead) (Downscourt Road). Maintain direction for 2.6 miles, passing roundabout and turn right in Selsdon at crossroad into Old Farleigh Road. After 1.6 miles turn left into Farleigh Court Road and continue for 0.6 miles and turn right into Farleigh Close for Farleigh church (372601) (A).

➠ **CYCLISTS: route starts here**

➠ Retrace steps and turn right, continue for 1.1 miles and turn left at a T-junction. After 0.6 miles turn right at the T-junction (signposted Warlingham and Limpsfield). In 0.1 miles turn left and immediate right (signposted Beddlestead, Tatsfield). Continue for 2.4 miles and turn left (signposted Westerham). In 0.1 miles turn right and after 0.5 miles turn left at a T-junction. Follow road round for 1.4 miles to Limpsfield (405532) (B).

➠ Continue to the main A25 and turn right (signposted Redhill). After 1.4 miles turn left (signposted Old Oxted) and in 0.2 miles left again just past Old Bell Inn (signposted Hurst Green). Continue for 0.9 miles and where road goes to the right continue straight on (signposted Crowhurst and Edenbridge). Maintain direction for 2.1 miles, cross railway and turn immediate left (signposted Crowhurst, Lingfield). Continue for 0.5 miles to Crowhurst church (391475) (C).

➠ Continue for 1.8 miles and at the T-junction turn right (signposted Godstone, East Grinstead). Pass Hare and Hounds Inn and in 0.6 miles turn left at T-junction (signposted Lingfield, East Grinstead). In 0.7 miles arrive at Lingfield Cage (386435) (D).

➠ Follow road round for 0.2 miles and turn left into Church Road (signposted Collegiate Church), continue for 0.1 miles to Lingfield church (389437) (E).

➠ Turn left out of church into Church Road and continue for 0.5 miles to a T-junction, and turn left (signposted Crowhurst, Godstone – Crowhurst Road). After 0.2 miles turn right (signposted to Haxted, Edenbridge) into Lingfield Common Road. In 2.1 miles turn left, just past Haxted Mill, into Dwelly Lane (signposted for Oxted, Limpsfield). In 1.5 miles turn right (signposted Edenbridge, Marlpit Hill). In 0.2 miles turn left (signposted Pains Hill, Limpsfield Chart). In 0.5 miles turn right (signposted Crockham Hill). In 0.7 miles turn left (signposted Itchingwood Common). In 1.0 miles turn right (signposted Crockham Hill). Continue for 1.1 miles and turn left on to the B2026 (signposted Crockham Hill, Westerham). In 1.1 miles turn right into Goodley Stock Road (signposted Westerham) and continue for 1.3 miles to Squerryes Court (440536) (F).

➠ Continue to the A25 and turn left for the M25 and London.

REFRESHMENTS

1. The Bell – in Limpsfield village south of the church (406530)

2. The Wheatsheaf

3. The Crown Inn

4. The George Inn

5. The Old Bell Inn – all in High Street Old Oxted (385524)

6. The Hare and Hounds – between Crowhurst and Lingfield but nearer Lingfield (387447)

7. The Old Cage

8. The Greyhound Inn

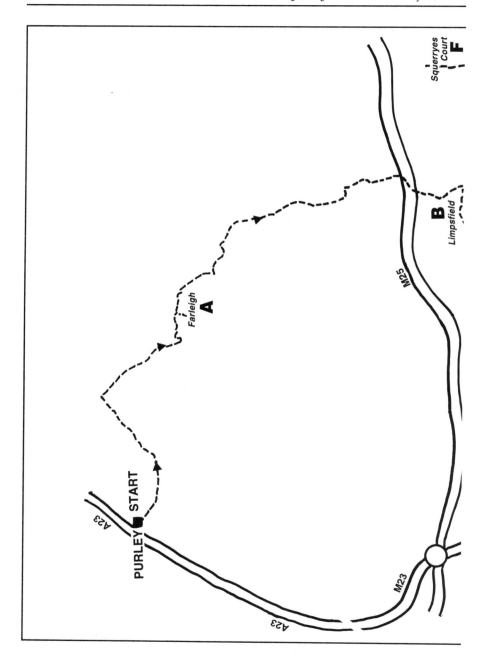

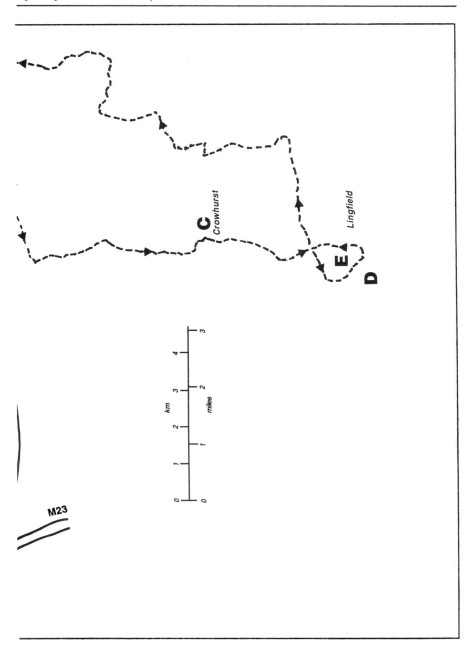

9. Best Wishes Tea Room

10. The Star – all in Lingfield (386436)

11. The Royal Oak – on B2026 in Crockham Hill between Lingfield and Westerham (443506)

7: Local Heroes: Pitt, Wilberforce, Darwin, Wolfe and Churchill

Route: West Wickham – Keston – Downe – Chevening – Westerham – Biggin Hill

Distance: 32 miles/51 km

West Wickham

Set on the edge of suburbia, the church of St. John the Baptist, West Wickham, and the adjacent Wickham Court have a definite foot in the countryside, and there are genuine rural views to the west of the churchyard.

After the Conquest, the manor was held by Odo, Bishop of Bayeux. It later came into the hands of the Bullen (Boleyn) family and was reputedly a meeting place for Anne Boleyn and Henry VIII.

Sir Henry Heyden built both the 15th century flint church and the impressive red brick and turretted Wickham Court. The house has octagonal corner turrets, a low west porch and renewed 19th century mullioned windows. After becoming a hotel it later became a Roman Catholic training college and is now Schiller International University.

Keston

Near to Keston is Caesar's Well, where legend tells us that Julius Caesar camped. It is here that the Ravensbourne River rises. It enters the

Thames at Deptford but is dammed at Keston to form three large and attractive ponds, with parking nearby. Close by is a weatherboarded post mill, dated 1716.

William Pitt the Younger lived nearby at Holwood, a house built for him by Sir John Soane. It was here that William Wilberforce came in 1788 and resolved to hasten the abolition of the slave trade – the visit being commemorated by an inscription on a stone seat. The seat can be seen by walking a few hundred yards south from the car park by the ponds and then taking the footpath to the left. The inscription reads "I well remember, after a conversation with Mr. Pitt, in the open air, on the root of an old tree at Holwood, just above the steep descent into the Vale of Keston, I resolved to give notice, on a fit occasion, to bring forth the abolition of the slave trade". The old oak tree still stands – just. It is a mere fragment and held up with supports.

Downe

It was to Downe that Charles Darwin came in 1842 where for years he researched his monumental and revolutionary work "On the Origin of Species by Means of Natural Selection". His home was Downe House, an 18th century building just to the south of the village and now open to the public.

Charles Robert Darwin was born in the Midlands, at Shrewsbury in 1809. He was fascinated by nature as a child and he and his brother, Erasmus, collected insects and carried out chemistry experiments in an improvised laboratory housed in the garden tool-shed. His formal education was first at the University of Edinburgh and later Christ's College, Cambridge. For him, however, this was not a fruitful time. He wrote later " . . . during the three years which I spent at Cambridge, my time was wasted, as far as the academical studies were concerned, as completely as at Edinburgh and at school".

Later he sailed on HMS Beagle, a ship engaged to survey the South American coast, and in 1839 married his first cousin, Emma Wedgwood. They moved to Downe House with their two children, William and Anne Elizabeth, in 1842.

At Downe House, Darwin wrote many books, including a treatise on Coral Reefs, Volcanic Islands and the Geology of South America, but his most famous work was, of course, "The Origin of Species", published in 1859.

The house is now owned by the Royal College of Surgeons. Darwin apparently disliked the house – commenting "House ugly, looks neither old or new, walls two feet thick, windows rather small, lower storey rather low".

Charles Darwin died in 1882 and is buried in Westminster Abbey.

Chevening

Chevening is a tiny hamlet, secluded and remote but within the roar of the nearby M25. It consists of Chevening House, the church of St Botolph, and a group of estate cottages. In one of these modest cottages, opposite to the church, lived Arabella Thrale, the daughter of Dr Johnson's friend. The church is 13th century but has a 15th century tower with stair turret in the north-east corner.

At the end of the lane is the entrance to Chevening House – most definitely not open to the public. The house was built for Richard Lennard, the thirteenth Earl Dacre in the early 17th century by, it is said, Inigo Jones. It was later purchased by General James Stanhope, Foreign Secretary and Head of Government to George I in 1717.

The Stanhope family was known for the eccentricity of two of its members. First there was Charles, the third Earl. He married William Pitt's sister and was well-known for his republican leanings. He found himself in a minority of one when he acknowledged the French Republic in Parliament and was thenceforth known as "Minority of One" and "Citizen Stanhope". He was also something of a scientist and invented all manner of devices, including a mathematical contraption to multiply and divide and an iron printing press. He also launched "the first little craft ever propelled by steam" on the lake in Chevening Park.

His daughter, Lady Hester Stanhope, was a similarly unique character. A disagreement with her father prompted her to go and live and keep house at Downing Street with her uncle, William Pitt the Younger. She was an extremely forceful and dominant lady and Pitt was resigned to this – "I let her do as she pleases; for if she were resolved to cheat the devil she could do it". On Pitt's death in 1806 she received a State pension of £1200 per year which she used to travel, finally settling in the Lebanon where she continued in her autocratic ways, having a firm hand over the local Druse people.

The seventh Earl Stanhope died in 1969, at which time the house was put in trust under condition that it should be occupied only by the Prime Minister, a Cabinet Minister, a member of the Royal Family descended from George VI, the Canadian High Commissioner, or the United States Ambassador.

Prince Charles has lived here for a short while, but his stay was not long. Neither, for that matter, was it for some of Mrs. Thatcher's ministers.

A view from Chevening Church

Westerham

Westerham was the birthplace and boyhood home of Major General James Wolfe – the victor at Quebec, and at nearby Chartwell lived Sir Winston Churchill. Both are commemorated on Westerham's splendid triangular village green. The bronze statue of Wolfe, by Derwent Wood (1911) is inscribed "Major General James Wolfe born at Westerham January 2nd 1727 died at Battle of Quebec 13 September 1759". The large bronze statue of Churchill was a gift from Yugoslavia and is inscribed "The plinth was presented by Marshal Tito and the people of Yugoslavia as a symbol of Yugoslav soil, in homage to Sir Winston Churchill's leadership in the war, 23 July 1969".

The church at Westerham lies at the eastern end of the green and contains many items of interest. James Wolfe was baptised in the octagonal font and beneath the tower on its north wall are the arms of Edward VI – Henry VIII's only son. Also within the tower is a remarkable wooden spiral staircase dating from the 14th century.

The main street descends towards the east with Quebec House – the boyhood home of Wolfe – at the bottom on the left. But first, on the right, there is the imposing Grosvenor House, an early 18th century house with large pilasters at the corners and a Doric pilaster to the doorcase.

Quebec House is brick with three gables on each facade. It was built around 1526 and in Wolfe's time was known as Spiers. It was acquired by Joseph Bowles Learmont of Montreal in 1913 and given to the National Trust in 1918.

Wolfe's parents moved from York to rent Spiers in 1726. James Wolfe was born at the nearby Vicarage, but Spiers was his home until the family moved to Greenwich in 1738. Wolfe was given his first commission at 14 years of age. He was present at the defeat of the Young Pretender at the Battle of Culloden, served in the Netherlands and later in Ireland as Quartermaster General. At this time he was critical of the Government. "The country is going fast upon its ruin – by the paltry projects and more ridiculous execution of those who are entrusted." In the late 1750s, Wolfe's career moved rapidly forward. He defeated the French at Louisbourg, Cape Breton, in Canada in 1758. He was again in

Canada in 1759 – this time for his most famous victory. On 13th September, 1759, 4500 men occupied the Heights of Abraham above Quebec and here defeated the French under Montcalm. Wolfe was shot in the chest and mortally wounded. "Now I die contented" he exclaimed, with a smile on his face.

James Wolfe was buried in Greenwich parish church on the 20th November, 1759, and at Quebec House are a fine collection of personal relics of Wolfe and exhibits of the battle at Quebec.

Biggin Hill

Biggin Hill, named after John Byggyn, a 16th century landowner, is famous as an RAF fighter station and renowned as a base for Spitfires in the Battle of Britain. There used to be a Hurricane and a Spitfire fighter plane at the main entrance to commemorate past glories, but when I was last there all that remained was one Spitfire.

Biggin Hill is now a civil airport for business and club flying.

Second World War Spitfire, Biggin Hill

ROUTE

(Cyclists should note that rather more of this route is along main roads compared with other chapters)

⊪➤ Join the A21 north from the M25 (junction 4) or south-east from Bromley, and continue to Locksbottom where join the A232 (signposted Croydon). After 2.5 miles turn left at roundabout for the A2022 (signposted Addington, Selsdon). In 0.2 miles turn left at roundabout into Layham Road and in 0.1 miles turn right for Wickham Court (389648) (A).

⊪➤ **CYCLISTS: route starts here**

⊪➤ Return to Layham Road and turn right and continue for 1 mile and turn left into North Pole Lane. In 0.5 miles turn left at a T-junction and then in 0.3 miles turn right at T-junction. After 0.1 miles turn left into Fox Lane and continue for 0.3 miles to main road, where you turn right by the Fox public house. Continue for 0.6 miles past the windmill on the right to the T-junction and turn left into Westerham Road. Continue for 0.3 miles to car park on left at Keston Ponds (419641) (B).

⊪➤ Retrace steps on the A233 for 0.9 miles and turn left into Downe Road (signposted Downe, High Elms). In 0.2 miles follow road around to the right and in 1.1 miles follow road to right at Downe church. Continue for 0.4 miles along Luxted Lane to Downe House (432612) (C).

⊪➤ Continue for 1.3 miles and turn left into Berry's Hill (signposted Cudham). In 0.1 miles follow road to the left, and in 0.6 miles turn right at the T-junction and immediate right. Maintain direction for 2.2 miles to T-junction and turn right. In 0.5 miles turn left and continue for 0.6 miles to T-junction and turn right. After 1.1 miles turn left at T-junction (signposted Chevening, Chipstead, Dunton Green). After 0.4 miles turn left and continue to Chevening church (489577) (D).

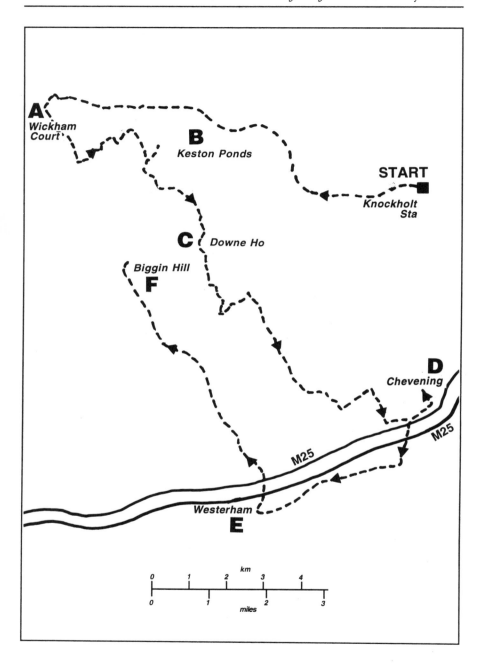

➠Retrace steps to T-junction and turn right (signposted Sundridge, Brasted, Westerham). Continue, cross M25, and after 1.2 miles turn right at traffic lights by White Horse public house on to the A25 (signposted Westerham). Continue for 2.6 miles to Westerham (447541) (E).

➠Turn right in Westerham on to the A233 for 5.2 miles to Biggin Hill (410605) (F).

➠Continue ahead for London, or return to Westerham and turn left for the M25 (east) or right for the M25 (west).

REFRESHMENTS

1. The Fox

2. The Greyhound – both in Keston (414645)

3. The Queens Head

4. The George and Dragon – both in Downe village (433616)

5. The Blacksmiths Arms – in Cudham village between Downe and Chevening (445598)

6. The White Horse – on A25 in Sundridge (482553)

7. The White Hart

8. The Village Tea Room

9. The Kings Arms

10. The Bull Inn – all on the A25 in Brasted (472552)

11. The Old House at Home

12. Tiffins (café)

13. Tudor Rose (café)

14. Grasshopper Inn

15. The George and Dragon

16. The Kings Arms Hotel – all in Westerham (446540)

8: A Gothick Folly and an Indian Guru

Route: Plaxtol – Hadlow – West Peckham – Mereworth – Offham

Distance: 24 miles/38 km

Plaxtol

Hidden in a narrow lane three miles south of Wrotham is Old Soar Manor House. It is now administered by English Heritage. The manor house was built in 1290, but on the site of the former hall now stands Old Soar, a house of 1740. This leaves the solar, chapel and garderobe of the original manor house, which is open to the public. Beneath is a vaulted undercroft with stairs to the solar with its timber tie beam roof. The chapel has a 14th century piscina. Old Soar Manor House was once in the hands of the Culpeper family.

Further along the lane is the chequered brick house, Broadfield, dated 1700.

Further on, we come to the attractive mediaeval half-timbered Spout House. This is now a showroom for the art metalwork factory next to it.

Hadlow

The area around Hadlow is flat, and so the Gothic tower, built as a folly by W.B. May in 1838, is something of a landmark and can be seen for miles around. It was originally part of Hadlow Court Castle and built to outdo the similar tower that William Beckford had built for himself at

Spout House, Plaxtol

Fonthill in Wiltshire. The architect was George Ledwell Taylor, engineer and architect to the navy. The tower is 170 ft in height with gables, crockets and pinnacles. Legend says that May constructed the tower to keep a watch over his estranged wife. Others say it was to get a view of the sea. In the Second World War it was used as a watch tower.

Hadlow Court Castle was demolished in 1951 but remains of the gateways and lodges can be seen in the main street, on the right.

Church Street is the most attractive corner of Hadlow village, with George House and Chancel House making an appealing group with the church.

St Mary's church has a Norman tower with Saxon long and short work at the base of its north east corner. Its most remarkable feature is the beautifully elaborate Coverdale chair. This was given in 1919 by T E Foster MacGeagh of Hadlow Court Castle and reputedly belonged to Miles Coverdale, Bishop of Exeter in 1551, and famous as translator of the Bible.

There is a poignant memorial in Hadlow churchyard. It reads "This monument was erected by public subscription in memory of thirty hop pickers who were drowned at Hartlake Bridge in a flood of the River Medway on 20th October 1853 and whose bodies are buried in this churchyard." "In the midst of life we are in death." The monument is in the south east corner of the churchyard and consists of a small pyramid on a square base. All the names of the victims are recorded and sixteen were from the same family – the Leatherlands. They were all crossing the River Medway in a wagon at nearby Hartlake Bridge on their way back to their camp at Tudley. The bridge collapsed and the wagon overturned, leaving the gypsies to be carried away and drowned in the flood currents.

West Peckham

West Peckham has what all good villages should have – a church, a cricket pitch and a pub.

The church of St Dunstan has a Saxon ragstone tower, but the main body of the church is 15th century. Its most notable feature is the Geary pew. This is reached from stairs to the north east of the chancel. On the upper level there is a large monument to Leonard Bartholomew and his wife, with a fine 17th century doorway to the main part of the pew, with open segmental pediment and carvings of fruit from a cartouche of arms. Constructed in the 17th century, the pew seats ten but it fell out of use in 1944 on the death of Sir William Geary.

During restoration of the church in 1887, plans were made to remove the steps leading to the pew. These were vigorously opposed by Sir Francis Geary and the matter went to law. The plaintiffs were the Vicar and Churchwardens and the case was heard in Consistory Court. Judgment was given in Sir Francis Geary's favour.

West Peckham's village green and church

Mereworth

On the left, on the way to Mereworth, is the handsome house Yotes Court. This red brick house was built for James Master in 1656. It has an H-plan construction, with two storeys and a hipped roof.

In the 1980s the protesting voices of the people of Kent were heard – at least to some extent – when they were presented with the prospect of the high-speed Channel railway link causing their homes to be demolished. This was not the case in the 1720s, however, when John Fane, later the seventh Earl of Westmorland, decided he wanted to build a Palladian mansion, with extensive grounds, on the site of Mereworth village. The old village, with its mediaeval church, was to the south of the present-day village and it interfered with the Earl's plans. Fane's solution was simple: he merely demolished the old village and built a new one. The mediaeval church upset the symmetry of the Palladian mansion and so it, along with the village, was knocked down "because it was an ancient building and most inconvenient".

The whole business has been quoted as "aristocratic arrogance", and I suppose it may have been at the time, but what we are left with now is unique in Kent. A grand and noble church, which would not be out of place in the City of London, and the spectacular Mereworth Castle.

The church of St Lawrence, with its soaring steeple, is something of a local landmark. Horace Walpole commented " . . . the new church with a steeple which seems designed for the latitude of Cheapside and is so tall that the poor church curtsies under it . . . ". It is modelled on three London churches. The main body is from St Paul's, Covent Garden. The spire is taken from James Gibbs' St Martin's in the Fields, while the western portico is inspired by Thomas Archer's St Paul's, Deptford. There is much controversy concerning the identity of the architect. Some say it was Colen Campbell, who designed Mereworth Castle, while others attribute it to James Gibbs or Thomas Archer. But the most likely is Roger Morris (1695 to 1749), an assistant of Campbell, who also designed the Palladian Marble Hill House at Twickenham. The church is entered through the semi-circular western portico of Ionic columns leading to the Tuscan nave. There are Doric columns, a barrel vaulted ceiling and a plaster ceiling to the aisles. The west gallery, supported by iron pillars, contains the Mereworth pew. The tower is surmounted by lantern and spire. Beneath it are monuments transferred from the old mediaeval church.

Mereworth has associations with the Crimean War admirals Sir William Hall and Charles Davis Lucas. On 21st June, 1854, Hall was commanding the paddle-steamer Hecla and Lucas served under him as Mate. Hecla was part of the British Fleet attacking batteries at Aland Island, Finland, and during the ferocious engagement an unexploded shell fell on to the deck of the ship. With blind disregard for his own safety, Lucas picked the lighted shell from the deck and tossed it into the sea – thereby saving the ship and its crew from certain disaster. His bravery was rewarded – he later became an Admiral; he married Sir William Hall's daughter and was the first recipient of the Victoria Cross.

In 1720, John Fane, MP and Chancellor of Oxford University, started building Mereworth Castle at a cost of £100,000. His architect was Colen Campbell, who based his design on Palladio's Villa del Capra, near Vicenza. The work was finished in 1748. In 1752 Horace Walpole was to visit: "Since dinner, we have been to Lord Westmorland's at Mereworth, which is so perfect in a Palladian taste, that I must own it has recovered me a little from Gothic. It is better situated than I had expected from the bad reputation it bears . . . The design, you know, is taken from the Villa del Capra by Vicenza, but on a larger scale; yet though it has cost £100,000, it is still only a fine villa; the finishing of in and outside has been exceedingly expensive . . . " The castle is difficult to see, but the grey dome and the Ionic columns to the portico can be glimpsed from the A26 (drive with care!). To the left, here, are the lodges to the castle. To the rear (and clearly visible from the lane) is a ruined triumphal arch, with massive columns and Corinthian capitals.

A little further on is the warm and appealing Roydon Hall, now the centre for Transcendental Meditation. Built in 1535, it has an archway to its entrance with octagonal turrets at its ends.

Roydon Hall

At the time of the Civil War and Commonwealth, Roydon Hall was owned by Sir Roger Twysden, who frequently fell out with parliament. He and another were summoned to the House of Commons in 1642 to explain themselves. A wit wrote:

*"Ask me not why The House delights
Not in our two wise Kentish Knights;
Their counsel was never thought good
Because they were not understood."*

North of Mereworth Woods lies the clean and pleasant village of Offham.

Offham

Offham's main claim to fame is its quintain (or tilting post), which stands on the village green. The quintain is made up of an upright and a crossbar. The crossbar turns on a swivel, one end of which is a sturdy board and the other carries a heavy bag of sand. The height of the crossbar above the ground is equivalent to the height of a man's head when on horseback. The idea was for the tilter to hit the broad end of the crossbar with his staff – but ride swiftly by before the sandbag swung round and struck him. The sport dates from Roman times and

The Quintain at Offham

was most popular in mediaeval days. It is best described in *Highways and Byways*: ". . . he that by chance hit it not at all, was treated with loud peals of derision, and he who did hit it made the best use of his swiftness, lest he should have a sound blow on his neck from the bag of sand, which instantly swung round from the other end of the quintain. The great design of this sport was to try the agility of the horse and man and to break the board, which whoever did he was accounted chief of the day's sport". Walter Jerold, who wrote *Highways and Byways* in Kent, then makes the social comment: "It would be a healthier exercise for the youth of today than watching other youths play football". This was back in 1907! Nothing changes, and life goes on!

There are two splendid houses in Offham. First, by the green, is Quintain House. It was built around 1700 and is of chequered red and blue brick with a hipped roof. Further east is Manor House, this of purple brick with red dressings. It has a fine pedimented doorcase with attached fluted columns.

North of the village is the diminutive church of St Michael and All Angels. The building consists of nave, chancel and tower – it is Norman but with 13th and 15th century additions. There is a Norman window on the north side of the nave.

The name Offham itself signifies an Anglo-Saxon village, for it derives from the Saxon name *Offa* and *ham*, a village.

ROUTE

➡ Leave the M20 at junction 2A (Wrotham) and follow the signs for Paddock Wood. After 0.5 miles turn right at the A25 (signposted Sevenoaks).

➡ **CYCLISTS: route starts here**

➡ In 0.1 miles turn left into Windmill Hill. After 0.8 miles, turn right and then immediately left into Beechin Wood Lane (signposted Crouch, Plaxtol). In 0.5 miles at first junction carry straight ahead to join Long Mill Lane, i.e. join road coming in from the right. Continue for 0.9 miles where bear left into The Hurst (signposted Old Soar Manor) and then in 0.5 miles turn right (signposted Old Soar). Continue for 0.2 miles to Old Soar (619541) (A).

➡ Continue for 0.2 miles past Broadfield and in 0.2 miles turn right into Brook Lane (signposted Plaxtol). In 0.2 miles turn left for Spout House (612536) (B).

➡ Take the immediate left to Long Mill Lane (signposted Dunks Hill, Tonbridge). After 0.7 miles, follow the road round to the right at the Kentish Rifleman into Dunks Green Road. At crossroad, after 0.3 miles, turn left into Hampton Road (signposted West Peckham, Hadlow, Maidstone). Maintain direction for 1.6 miles and then turn right for Hadlow. After 0.9 miles, turn left at a T-junction (A26) into Hadlow (signposted Mereworth, Maidstone). In 0.1 miles turn right into Church Street for Hadlow church (635497) (C).

➡ Leave Church Street and turn right on to the A26 and continue for 0.7 miles then turn left (signposted Plaxtol, Shipbourne). In 0.1 miles turn right into Matthews Lane (signposted West Peckham, Borough Green). In 1 mile turn right. After 0.4 miles at junction keep right (signposted West Peckham, Mereworth) and in 0.1 miles turn right for West Peckham green and church (645525) (D).

➡ Retrace steps from West Peckham church, turn right and continue on Mereworth Road for 0.7 miles to crossroads where keep straight on for 0.4 miles to Mereworth church (660537) (E).

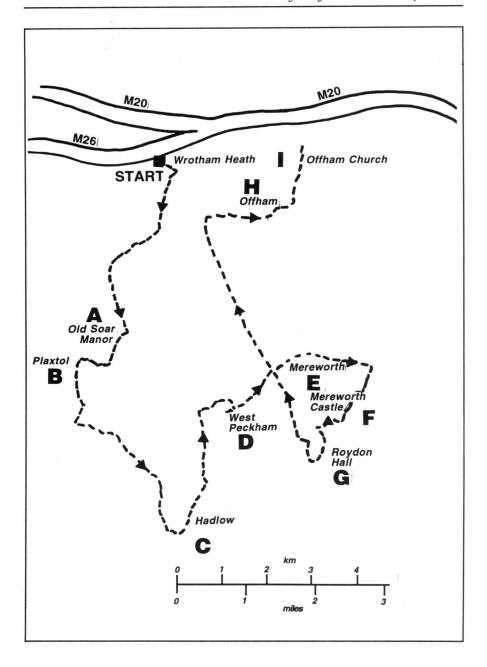

➡ Continue for 0.1 miles to crossroads, cross main road (signposted Maidstone A26) and in 0.1 miles join the A26. After 0.4 miles pass the lo(˙ ᴉe and entrance to Mereworth Castle. In a further 0.4 miles turn riɡ into Pizien Well Road at Mulligans Fish Restaurant. In 0.4 miles turn right into Park Road. Continue for 0.6 miles past Triumphal Arch Mereworth Castle (668523) (F).

➡ In 0.3 miles turn left, and in 0.2 miles pass Roydon Hall (665516) (G).

➡ In a further 0.3 miles turn right at main road. At roundabout in 0.9 miles take the B2016 (signposted Wrotham, London, Motorways). In 2.8 miles turn right into Comp Lane (signposted Offham, West Malling) and continue for 1.2 miles to Offham (657573) (H).

➡ Go north from Offham Green along North Meadow (signposted Offham Church, Addington). In 0.1 miles join road coming in from the right, and continue for 0.5 miles to Offham church (660581) (I).

➡ Continue ahead from Offham church, turn left at the A20 for the M20, M25 and London.

REFRESHMENTS

1. The Chequers Inn – early in the route at Crouch hamlet before Old Soar (617555)

2. The Kentish Rifleman – between Old Soar Manor and Hadlow south of Plaxtol (613526)

3. The Rose and Crown

4. The Blacksmiths Arms

5. The Fiddling Monkey

6. The Harrow – all in Hadlow village (635497)

7. The Swan – opposite the green in West Peckham village (645524)

8. The Kings Arms – in Offham village (655574)

9: The Man who Banned Birdsong, and the Priest who Profited from Holy Water

Route: Otford – Shoreham – Kemsing – Wrotham – Ridley – Ash

Distance: 25 miles/40 km

Otford

Otford probably takes its name from 'Otta's ford'. Archbishop Warham's ruined palace is the principal place of interest, but Otford's history goes back much further than that. The Anglo-Saxon Chronicle tells us that in AD 774 "there appeared in the heavens a red crucifix after sunset; the Mercians and the men of Kent fought at Ottanford and wonderful serpents were seen in the land of the South Saxons". King Aldic of Kent lost the battle to Offa, King of the Mercians, and we are told that the "Darent ran red with Saxon blood".

Later, in 1016, Edmund Ironside defeated Canute and the Danes at Otford, but his victory was shortlived, for at the battle of Ashingdon in Essex later that year Canute was crowned King of England.

The palace at Otford has associations with Thomas Becket. He is reputed to have struck his staff on the ground and so produced the water supply – now seen as a small stream south of the remains. The Elizabethan historian, William Lambarde, writes of Becket's 'ban' on birdsong at

Otford: "As Thomas Becket walked on a time in the Olde Parke (busie at his prayers), that he was much hindered in devotion by the sweete note and melodie of a nightingale that sang in a bush beside him, and that therefore (in the might of his holynesse) he enjoined that from henceforth no byrde of that kynde should be so bolde as to sing thereaboutes". As if that was not enough, he is also supposed to have cursed a blacksmith who pricked his horse while shoeing it – and so prevented any smith from flourishing in the parish.

The remains of the palace, visible today, are a monument to Archbishop Wareham. Originally a large courtyard house, the northwest tower still stands where Thomas Cranmer is reputed to have written the "Book of Common Prayer". There is a shorter tower at the opposite end, and between a row of later cottages built on the remains of the palace walls. Cranmer gave the palace to Henry VIII. He wasn't fond of it and described it as "rheumatic like unto Croydon . . . where I could never be without sickness". The palace was used as a residence for Henry's daughter, Princess Mary – but later fell into disuse.

Shoreham

Shoreham is noted for its imposing cross, cut into the turf of the chalk downs. It commemorates the dead of two World Wars. On the right, as the river is approached, is the Kings Arms, complete with ostler's box. The ostler's job was to care for the horses while their owners were drinking at the inn, and he is seen inside as a wax figure. The box has windows to both road and bar to give the ostler sight of both the horse and his master.

Overlooking the Darent is Water House. It was here that the artist Samuel Palmer stayed from 1827 – 1834 and gave hospitality to William Blake. The architecture at Shoreham is small in scale but appealing, particularly the red brick Riverside House of 1774 and Flint Cottage.

A pathway lined with yew trees leads to the church, with its sturdy late perpendicular timber porch and tower of 1775. John Wesley was a frequent preacher here. Inside there is a handsome 16th century oak rood screen filling the entire width of the church, and an 18th century organ case and 19th century pulpit, both from Westminster Abbey.

To the left of the door, on the west wall, is a painting by Charles Cope. It shows the homecoming of Verney Cameron to Shoreham in 1875. Cameron was a great explorer who travelled to Africa to search (in vain) for Livingstone. He was the first white man to cross that continent. While there, he surveyed Lake Tanganyika, the Congo and the Zambesi. Cameroon, the West African state, takes its name from him.

Kemsing

In the centre of Kemsing village is St Edith's Well. St Edith was the daughter of King Edgar the Peaceful and Lady Wulfrith. She was born here in 961 but spent most of her short life as a nun at Wilton. As was the practice in the Middle Ages, a shrine was set up to her and this attracted people journeying on the Pilgrims Way to Canterbury.

Local people also came to have their corn blessed by the priest at Kemsing in St Edith's name. For a price, mildew and blight were kept at bay.

Lambarde viewed the business with some cynicism, and wrote at length:

"The manner of the sacrifice was this: Some silly body brought a peck, or two, or a bushel of corn, to the church: and (after prayers made) offered it to the Image of the Saint: of this Offering the Priest used to toll the greatest portion, and then to take one handful, or little more of the residue

St Edith's well

*(for you must consider he would be sure to gain by the bargain) the
which after aspertion of holy water, and mumbling of a few words of
conjuration, he first dedicated to the image of St Edithe, and then
delivered it back to the party that brought it: who then departed with full
perswersion, that if he mingled that hallowed handfull with his seed
corn, it would preserve from harm, and prosper in growth, the whole
heap that he should sowe, were it never so great a Stack or Mough."*

Not only was corn protected, but the water of the well was supposed to
cure bad eyes.

The shrine was originally in the churchyard – enclosed now by a fine
crinkle-crankle wall – but it fell into disuse during the 16th century
because of concerns about idolatry.

Wrotham

Motorways and main roads surround Wrotham, but the village is now
happily free of traffic. From the village square, High Street runs to the
west with the plain, red brick and Georgian West House at its end. High
up and overlooking the square is the church of St George. Beneath the
15th century tower is a three-bay, rib vaulted passage. This acted as a
processional way and enabled the congregation to circle the church
without departing from consecrated land. The church has a large east
window which was brought from St Albans, Wood Street, in the City of
London, and installed here in 1958. It was designed by Sir Christopher
Wren and was originally the west window of the City church.

On the opposite side of the square is the Elizabethan Wrotham Place,
with mullioned and transomed windows. In former times the Archbishop of Canterbury had a manor at Wrotham, sited to the east of the
church. It fell into disuse under Archbishop Islip in the 14th century.

Ridley

Ridley is remote and peaceful. The tiny hamlet has a small turretted
church and an 18th century house. There is a Norman window in the
nave of the church and the 18th century Court Farm House has a fine
hipped roof.

Ash

Ash is similarly remote. The church, manor house and cricket pitch make an ideal group in quiet downland off the main road. The manor house is dated 1637, is of red brick, three storeys, and with a gabled porch.

The cricket ground at Ash

ROUTE

➠ From the M25 (junction 5) join the A21 (signposted Sevenoaks). Take the first left turn to join the A25 (signposted Sevenoaks). Remain on the A25 through Riverhead, and at the first set of traffic lights turn left on to the A225 for Otford (signposted Dartford Tunnel, Farningham). After 1.7 miles turn left at Otford roundabout and park in car park opposite the Bull Inn. Return on foot to the roundabout and take the footpath to the right of the church (signposted Sevenoaks Road) to Otford Palace (526594) (A).

➠ **CYCLISTS: route starts here; note that the route is linear.**

➠ Turn right out of car park, leave Otford and after passing under railway bridge turn right. After a short while take the right fork, cross railway and continue to Shoreham, and turn right (the Royal Oak pub). The Kings Arms is on the right as enter Shoreham village (520616) (B).

➠ Continue through Shoreham to the A225 and turn right and after 0.5 miles turn left into Fackenden Lane. After 1 mile turn left up narrow lane, and then after 1.4 miles join lane coming in from the right. At crossroads turn right for Kemsing. After 200 yards, turn right at the Y-junction. Continue straight on, through two sets of crossroads and at T-junction turn right (signposted Kemsing). After 0.6 miles turn right for car park at Kemsing (555587) (C).

➠ St Edith's well is in the centre of the village.

➠ Turn right out of the church car park, pass through Kemsing and take the first right into The Landway. At a T-junction turn right on to Pilgrims Way. Continue for 4.2 miles and at a T-junction (The Old Vicarage) turn left for Wrotham (612592) (D).

➠Continue through Wrotham and turn left at roundabout on to the A20, cross motorway. At the next roundabout turn right on to the A227 (signposted Gravesend). Take the first left after 0.2 miles. In 1 mile join the road coming in from the right (Vigo Road). After 0.5 miles turn right (signposted Ridley, Ash) in to Fairseat Lane, and left in 0.7 miles at T-junction (signposted Ridley, Ash). At the T-junction turn right and continue for 0.4 miles for Ridley (617639) (E).

➠Retrace route and straight on for 1 mile. Turn right at T-junction and after 0.3 miles turn right for Ash (603645) (F).

➠Retrace steps from Ash and turn right for London (via the A20) or the M25 (via the A20).

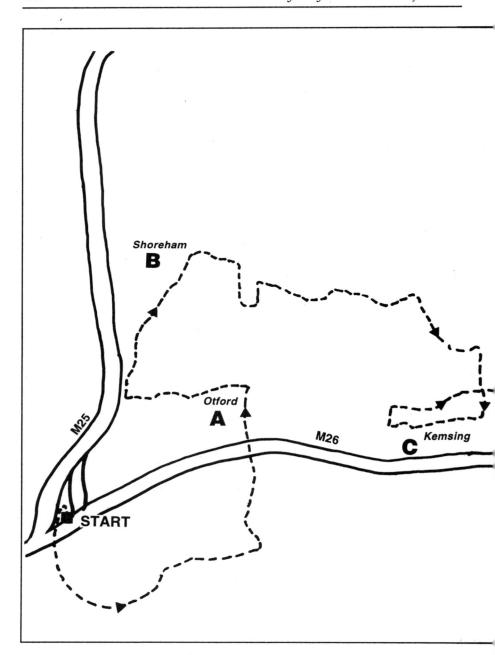

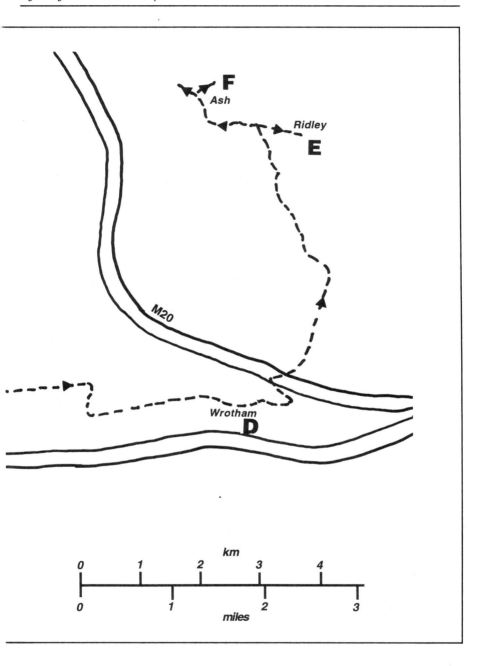

REFRESHMENTS

1. The Willow Room Café

2. The Woodman

3. The Crown

4. The Bull

5. The Horns – all in Otford (527594)

6. The Royal Oak

7. The Kings Arms

8. The Olde George – all in Shoreham (520616)

9. The Rising Sun – between Shoreham and Kemsing but much nearer to Kemsing (563599)

10. The Bell

11. The Wheatsheaf – both in Kemsing (555587)

12. The George and Dragon

13. The Rose and Crown

14. The Three Post Boys

15. The Bull Hotel – all in Wrotham (612592)

16. The White Swan – in Ash (turn right out of road leading from the church (597645)

10: Roman Recycling – and a Saxon Tower within Earshot of Brands Hatch

Route: Farningham – Eynsford – Lullingstone – West Kingsdowne – Darenth

Distance: 20 miles/32 km

Farningham

Motorways and by-passes surround Farningham, but the village itself is peaceful. It lies on the old London to Dover road and in the 18th century stage coaches used the Lion Hotel as a stopping point. It is a late 18th century inn, with a red brick front facing the River Darent, which flows across the main village street. The bridge is also 18th century and just downstream of it is a brick and flint folly of a bridge. Opposite is an excellent weather-boarded water flour mill with house behind.

Farningham is altogether pleasant – but fashions change. As late as 1948, Church in 'The County Guide' writes of Farningham: ". . . though heaven knows there is still not much to write home about" and "Farningham is now merely a London omnibus terminus . . . " . I would disagree with all that. I found it rewarding to walk along the village street. It leads to the 13th – 15th century church of St Peter and St Paul. In the churchyard there is an impressive mausoleum, probably designed by John Nash, to Thomas Nash who died in 1778. The story goes that in former days the girls of the village would throw pins into a hole in the mausoleum to induce the devil to make an appearance. Inside the church there is a fine octagonal font. Its panels are carved and there are only thirty fonts of this type in the whole country, all of them being in East Anglia with the exception of the one in Somerset at Nettlecombe. Starting with the panel on the west face, they depict first of all confirmation, with Bishop, child and Godparent. Then penance, with seated priest and kneeling penitent with the devil at the rear. After this, Holy Communion, with priest at the altar. Then there is the administration of Holy Communion. The fifth panel shows Extreme Unction with priest, dying man and an attendant, followed by Ordination, with the Bishop and candidate. Matrimony is next with priest, bride in 15th century headdress and bridegroom. Finally there is baptism, with priests, infant, Godmother and another person.

Bligh of the Bounty had his home at Farningham manor. He was a contemporary of Cook and was not exactly renowned for his skills as a man manager. So much so that his men were driven to mutiny while on a voyage from Tahiti to the West Indies. The mutinous men settled on the Pitcairn Islands and their descendants have remained there ever since.

The Lion Hotel and River Darent, Farningham

Eynsford

Eynsford is famous for its picturesque and much-photographed ford, providing a crossing point over the Darent.

The castle contains many re-used Roman tiles and is unique, for according to Pevsner: "Nowhere in England is there a more complete example of a pre-keep castle". It has an extremely wide and flat motte and was built around 1100. Later, a stone hall house was added at the north east corner. In the 12th century it was occupied by one William de Eynsford.

The church is of Norman origin with an apse at its east end and a 12th century Norman west door, with zigzag moulding. In 1163 a vacancy arose for a priest and the then Archbishop of Canterbury, Thomas Becket, appointed his own man to the position.

This wasn't to the liking of William de Eynsford, who promptly turned him out. Becket retaliated in customary manner by e x c o m m u n i c a t i n g William. The dispute serves to highlight the conflict between Henry II and Becket, for William was a member of Henry's Court, to whom he appealed to make the excommunication void. Henry objected to Becket, reasoning that he was in danger by consorting with an excommunicate,

Eynsford

arguing that " . . . since I have not been warned, and since my dignity has been injured in this essential point, the excommunication of my vassal is void".

Eynsford was the scene of experiments by Percy Pilcher, one of the pioneers of flight. He flew his bamboo glider from hilltop to hilltop late in the 19th century. His Hawk, as it was known, only weighed 50 lbs, but it once flew 250 yards. It was a monoplane with rear fin, tailplane and wheeled undercarriage. Pilcher controlled it by swinging himself from a hanging position between the wings. Its last flight was in Leicestershire, near Market Harborough, where it crashed in 1899.

Lullingstone

The road to Lullingstone passes underneath the large and impressive brick railway viaduct. Just beyond are the remains of one of the most important Roman villas in the country. The villa is housed within a modern museum building, with walkways provided, enabling people to view the remains. They were excavated in 1949 and there are five separate and distinct building periods. The first is AD 80 – 90 when the original villa was built near an Iron Age farm. Then at the end of the second century, a luxury villa was constructed. This was roofed with red and yellow tiles and had a bathing suite with under-floor heating. Some time after that the site fell into decay and by 280 it had reverted to a mere farmhouse. Then in the 4th century two fine mosaic floors were laid. These survive and are clearly visible from the walkways. One shows Jupiter disguised as a bull abducting Europa and two cupids, one of which is pulling Jupiter's tail. The other depicts Bellerophon on the winged horse, Pegasus, slaying the Chimera.

Christian influence is found in the final building stage with, in the late 4th century, the provision of a chapel and anteroom. The walls of the chapel were painted with the Christian Chi-Rho monogram and six figures with their arms stretched out in prayer. The chapel is unique in Britain and is the oldest known site of Christian worship in the country.

Further along the lane is Lullingstone Castle. Entrance is through the fine, red brick Tudor gatehouse, built in 1497. The house has a Queen Anne facade but was built in the reign of Henry VIII by Sir John Peche.

Sir John was much in favour, both with Henry VII and Henry VIII. He accompanied the latter in 1520 to the Field of the Cloth of Gold. He was fond of jousting and won a golden ring presented to him by Henry VII's daughter, the Princess Margaret. His jousting helmet may be seen in the house.

Lullingstone Castle

The church, with cupola and classical porch, stands on the lawn in front of the house. The beautiful north chapel was added by Sir John Peche and it contains his tomb and effigy. He was also responsible for the elaborate rood screen displaying the pomegranate badge of Queen Katharine of Aragon and the Rose of England. Both Henry VIII and Queen Anne were frequent visitors to Lullingstone – indeed, the stairheads of the hall staircase were made deliberately shallow to allow the overweight Queen to climb them without difficulty. The beautiful plaster ceiling of the church was also added at the time of Queen Anne.

Lullingstone Church

West Kingsdowne

The old Saxon church of St Edmund at West Kingsdowne lies secluded in Shipbourne Forest. The peace and tranquillity of the place contrasts sharply with the excitement and roar of the motor racing circuit at Brands Hatch, which is barely half a mile away.

The nave and flint tower of the church are both Saxon. Inside there is an attractive wall painting, dated about 1110, in the splays of the south window. It tells the story of Cain and Abel. On the left is the sacrifice of Cain and Abel and, on the right, Cain killing Abel.

There are also two appealing 14th century stained glass quatrefoils. One shows Christ in majesty and the other the crowned Virgin and child.

There is a yew tree by the west door of this fine old church that is 1000 years old and supposed to be the oldest in Kent.

West Kingsdowne Church

Darenth

Darenth takes its name from, and lies on, the River Darent. On the banks of the river was once a Roman villa. This cannot be seen now, for any remains are completely overgrown with brambles. The church of St Margaret, however, contains many Roman bricks taken from the site. It is of Saxon origin as evidenced by the window above the north door. The Saxon nave leads via steps to the chancel and the separate early Norman sanctuary. This is of two storeys with groined vault and three small stepped east windows. There is a splendid font, dated 1140, showing, as some say, incidents from the life of St Dunstan. Reading clockwise from the east, the first panel shows baptism by immersion, then a bearded man with dragon, a rampant lion, a griffin, Sagittarius, King David playing a harp, a mystical creature and, finally, a man with a crown.

ROUTE

➠ From junction 3 (M25) take the A20 eastbound (signposted Farningham and West Kingsdown). At the second roundabout turn right along the lane (signposted Farningham). At the T-junction (by the Chequers Inn) turn left for Farningham High Street (547670) (A) and park in the village.

➠ **CYCLISTS: route starts here**

➠ At the end of Farningham High Street turn right on to the A225 (Eynsford Road) and after 0.7 miles turn right (by the garage and opposite the Castle Hotel) to Eynsford castle (542657) (B).

➠ Return to the A225 and turn right. Take the first right, cross the river Darent and continue for 1 mile to Lullingstone Roman villa (529652) (C).

➠ Continue for 0.5 miles to Lullingstone castle (529644) (D).

➠ Return to Eynsford village and turn left on to the A225, then first right. Continue for 3.2 miles to crossroads and carry straight over (signposted Woodlands, Kemsing, West Kingsdown). After 200 yards bear right at the Y-junction and turn left at the first cross-roads (signposted West Kingsdown). Continue for 2.2 miles to the A20 (by the Portobello public house). Cross the A20 and after 0.3 miles turn left into unmade road for Kingsdown church (580634) (E).

➠ Return to main road and turn left. Take the third right (opposite Brands Hatch circuit) into Three Gates Road, cross motorway and two sets of crossroads. Turn left at the Y-junction into School Lane.At the T-junction turn right(near to the Bull Inn). Continue straight ahead for 0.7 miles and then sharp left over railway (signposted South Darenth). After a few yards turn right and continue straight on at crossroads. At a T-junction turn left and after 200 yards turn left into parking space at Darenth church (561714) (F).

➠ Turn left out of Darenth church, left on to the A225 and, at the first crossroads, turn right for London or the M25.

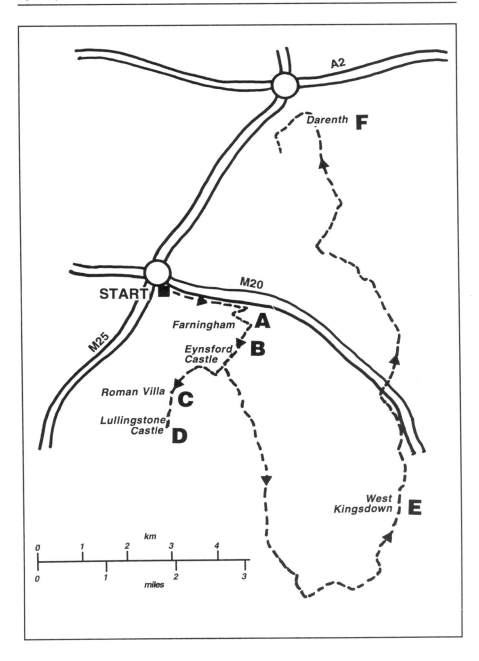

REFRESHMENTS

1. The Chequers Inn

2. The Lion Hotel

3. The Pied Bull – all in Farningham (546670)

4. The Castle Hotel

5. The Five Bells

6. Ford House Tea Shop

7. The Plough

8. Swallows Malt Shovel Inn – all in Eynsford (540655)

9. The Gatehouse Tea Room – within gatehouse of Lullingstone Castle (529645)

10. The Portobello – on the A20 in West Kingsdowne (580626)

11. The Bull – in Horton Kirby between West Kingsdowne and Darenth (563683)

11: Ashes to Ashes: Cricket, the Black Death and a Burial Chamber

Route: Cobham – Luddesdowne – Dode – Paddlesworth – Trottiscliffe

Distance: 18 miles/29km

Cobham

Cobham Hall, built in 1584 for the de Cobhams, is not normally open to the public. It is now a girls school. The Brooke family held the hall after the de Cobhams. In 1603 Henry Brooke, with Sir Walter Raleigh, attempted to install Lady Arabella Stuart to the throne instead of James I. For this he got life imprisonment and Cobham Hall passed to the Crown. It was later inherited by the Stuarts, cousins to the King, the most famous of whom was La Belle Stuart – Brittania on the original penny coins.

The Ashes, famous in cricket, used to be held at Cobham Hall. The story starts with the defeat of England by Australia at the Oval in 1882. The Sporting Times records: "The body will be cremated and the ashes taken to Australia". Following this, a group of Australian girls from Melbourne burnt a bail and put the ashes in an urn – hence the term. One of the girls was a Miss Morphy, who later married Ivo Bligh who, in the following year, captained the side that toured Australia and regained the Ashes.

Lord Downley, as he became, lived at Cobham Hall, which is where the Ashes were kept. There is a dreadful rumour that on one occasion during a ball at the Hall the Ashes were spilt by servants and that the butler refilled the urn with ashes from the fireplace. Scandalous!

Cobham is packed with interest and there is much to see. The church of St. Mary Magdalene has a noble chancel, built around 1220 with windows of the period and a delicate sedilia and piscina built a century later. Inside can be seen some of the finest brasses to be found anywhere in the country. They all commemorate the Cobham family, whose history is largely the history of Cobham itself. In the centre is the massive alabaster monument to Sir George Brooke, the ninth Lord Cobham. Surrounding him are his wife, ten sons and four daughters. When I was here last (Winter 1988) the floor of the chancel was boarded up because of redecoration and I was therefore unable to view the brass of Sir John de Cobham who rebuilt much of the church, including the tower, in the mid-14th century. His brass shows him holding in his hands the church he enlarged.

Sir John de Cobham was also responsible for building the college (now almshouses) to the south of the church. He was a contemporary of the

Cobham Church

Black Prince and also built Cooling Castle (see Chapter 12). The college is peaceful and quiet with beautifully mown grass in the quadrangle. It was built in 1362 and originally housed five priests who were required to say mass for the souls of Sir John's ancestors.

In 1598 the college was dissolved and the buildings became almshouses – and they remain so to this day. The original half of the college is at the south of the quadrangle. It is now the common room of the almshouses – but still retains its original roof and 15th century fireplace. South again are the remains of the south court. A kitchen was originally here, as evidenced by the fireplace. Above the doorway in the south wall are the Cobham Arms, complete with inscription, of 1598.

Historical associations are plentiful at Cobham. Charles Dickens is remembered at the Leather Bottle Inn for it was here that Mr. Tupman came in Pickwick Papers. The inn, restored after a fire in 1880, contains a large selection of paintings with a Dickensian theme.

The Leather Bottle Inn, Cobham

To the west of Cobham is Owletts. The house was built in 1683, is of five bays, two storeys, and has a fine hipped roof. Sir Herbert Baker lived here in 1917. The house passed to the National Trust in 1965.

Luddesdowne

By the church at Luddesdowne is Luddesdowne Court, which dates from Saxon times. The house is reputedly the oldest in continuous occupation in the whole of the country. At the time of William the Conqueror it was occupied by Odo, the Bishop of Bayeux.

Dode

Dode lies remote and isolated in woodland. The village people were wiped out in the Black Death of 1349 but their church of Norman origin remains. It was restored in 1910 and now belongs to the Roman Catholic Church. Outside there is a frighteningly deep well. Although it is (was) covered by a metallic grid, please keep your children away!

Paddleworth

Paddleworth, like Dode, was destroyed in the Black Death. It is also isolated, this time not in woodland but in open fields. The hamlet now consists of an 18th century red brick farmhouse and the Norman chapel which became redundant in 1637. The key can be obtained from the farmhouse opposite. Inside there is a western gallery and other fittings from the now demolished Holborough Court. Paddlesworth lies on the Pilgrims Way and would have been a stopping point for the Canterbury pilgrims just before the Medway crossing at nearby Snodland.

Trottiscliffe

Trottiscliffe is another village that suffered at the time of the Black Death. The Norman church of St Peter and St Paul and Court Lodge make a handsome group close to the foot of the Downs. On the site of the 18th century Court Lodge once stood a manor house of the Bishops of Rochester – but in 1348 thirty-two of Bishop Hamo de Hethe's people fell victim to the deadly plague.

The church has a fine interior – in particular the box pews and the reredos that depict on one side the Circumcision and on the other the Flight into Egypt. The pulpit is grand. It was originally in Westminster Abbey and was brought here in 1824. Its most impressive feature is the palm tree which supports the sounding board. There are Norman windows in the north and south walls of the chancel.

A short walk brings us to the famous Coldrum Long Barrow, a Neolithic burial chamber which was handed to the National Trust in 1926. Set in glorious countryside, it consists of four sandstone slabs positioned at the end of a mound.

ROUTE

➡ Leave the M25 at junction 2 and join the A2 (signposted Rochester and Dover). Continue for 8.8 miles after which turn left on to the B2009 (signposted Cobham, Shorne and Higham). At the T-junction turn left, cross over the A2 and a few yards to the left further on is the entrance to Cobham Hall (679696) (A).

➡ **CYCLISTS: route starts here**

➡ Proceed towards Cobham on the B2009. Turn left at T-junction (Halfpence Lane). After 0.7 miles, follow the road around to the right for Cobham Church and College (670685) (B) which is 0.3 miles further on, on the left.

➡ Continue for 0.4 miles for Owletts (665687) (C).

➡ Turn left at Owletts (signposted Sole Street). After 0.6 miles turn left into Gold Street (signposted Henley Street and Luddesdowne). After 0.3 miles turn right at the Y-junction, cross railway and continue to the Golden Lion public house, and turn right and continue for 0.3 miles to next junction, where you turn left for Luddesdown church (669662) (D).

➡ Return to the Golden Lion public house and turn sharp right for Great Buckland. After 0.5 miles join lane coming in from left. Continue for 1 mile and then take left fork (no through road) for Dode church (668637) (E) after 0.5 miles.

➡ Retrace route and after 0.5 miles turn sharp left. After 0.5 miles turn left (signposted Harvel). Continue to crossroads (the White Horse) and turn left (signposted Birling and Snodland). Continue for 1.9 miles and turn left into Paddleworth Road (signposted Paddleworth and Snodland) for, after 0.3 miles, Paddleworth church (684621) (F).

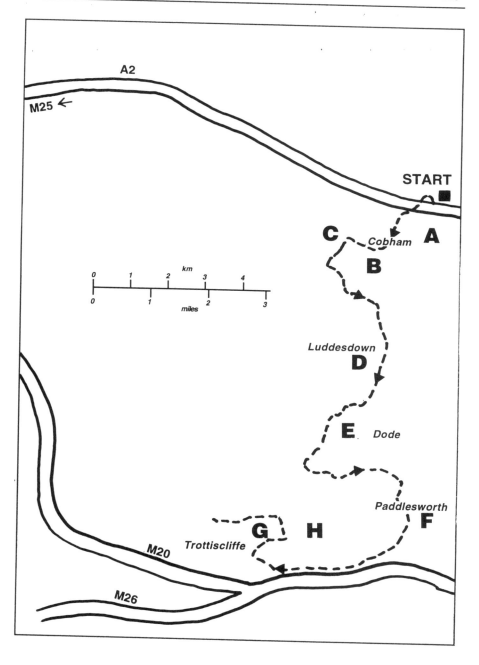

➥ Retrace steps for 0.3 miles to a T-junction, and turn left (signposted Birling and Ryarsh) into Stangate Road. Turn right at T-junction after 0.7 miles into Snodland Road. Continue for 2.2 miles through Birling and Ryarsh and turn right at the T-junction. After 0.9 miles turn right into School Lane just after the George public house in Trottiscliffe. After 0.5 miles turn left for Trottiscliffe church (646605) (G).

➥ Retrace steps from Trottiscliffe church and turn left. After 0.3 miles turn right for car park for Coldrum Long Barrow (649606) (H).Turn left at a T-junction, and then right at a T-junction for the A227, at which turn left for motorway system.

REFRESHMENTS

1. The Ship Inn

2. The Darnley Arms

3. The Leather Bottle – all in Cobham (672684)

4. The Cock Inn – between Cobham and Luddesdown (664673)

5. The Golden Lion – in Luddesdown before church (673665)

6. The Nevill Bull – in Birling village (between Paddlesworth and Trottiscliffe (680605)

7. The Duke of Wellington – in Ryarsh (between Paddlesworth and Trottiscliffe (670598)

8. The George – in Trottiscliffe village (642602)

12: The Dickens of a Journey: a two-mile Tunnel, the Isle of Grain and an Elizabethan Castle

Route: Higham – Cliffe – Cooling – Grain – Upnor – Higham

Distance: 33 miles/53km

Highham

Higham is rich in historical associations. Dickens lived here in his later years, and it is the scene of Falstaff's robbery in Shakespeare's Henry IV, Part I. There are remains of a canal and its tunnel, cut in the industrial revolution, and a remote and redundant church set apart in the remoteness of the Thames marshes.

On Gads Hill is the Sir John Falstaff Inn – commemorating the scene of the Sir John Falstaff robbery, and on the opposite side of the road is Gadshill Place, home of Charles Dickens from 1857 until his death in 1870. The house was built in 1779 and its mansard roof is surmounted by a cupola. Dickens knew the house when he was a boy living at nearby Chatham, and it was his father who seeded his imagination by remarking: "If you were to be persevering and were to work hard, you might some day come to live in it". And so it turned out, for Dickens purchased the house in 1856 for £1790. He wrote of his new home "At this present moment I am on my little Kentish freehold – looking on as pretty a view out of my study window as you will find in a long day's

English ride. My little place is a grave red brick house, which I have added to and stuck bits upon in all manner of ways, so that it is as pleasantly irregular and as violently opposed to all architectural ideas, as the most hopeful man could possibly desire. The robbery was committed before the door, on the man with the treasure, and Falstaff ran away from the identical spot of ground now covered by the room in which I write. A little rustic ale-house, called the Sir John Falstaff, is over the way – has been over the way ever since, in honour of the event . . . The whole stupendous property is on the old Dover road".

Some say the house was the home of Miss Havisham in Great Expectations. Hans Christian Andersen stayed there in 1857 as did Longfellow in 1868. Dickens remained at Gadshill Place until he died of a stroke in 1870.

The Sir John Falstaff Inn, Gadshill

The Sir John Falstaff Inn reminds us that in former days this was a dangerous place for travellers. It is immortalised in Shakespeare's Henry IV, Part I:

"But, my lads, my lads, tomorrow morning,
by four o clock, early at Gadshill.
There are pilgrims going to Canterbury
with rich offerings, and traders riding
to London with fat purses. "

This was not the only infamous robbery at Gadshill. Once, early one morning, a highwayman named Nick robbed a passer-by at this spot. He crossed the Thames at Gravesend and rode in haste to York to make good his escape. There, he was fortunate to meet the Lord Mayor in a bowling alley and thereby obtained the perfect alibi – that being, that it would have been impossible to thieve in Higham in the morning and be in York by afternoon. Dick Turpin's ride to York on Black Bess is taken from this story.

The cutting of the former Thames and Medway canal can be seen further north in Higham village by the railway station. The canal's purpose was to shorten the 47 mile journey that river traffic had to take between Gravesend and the Medway towns. It was begun in 1801 and what is now the Higham railway tunnel was originally the canal tunnel – the second longest in the country. It was originally proposed by Ralph Dodd whose idea was for a cutting through the chalk Downs – but this was later changed to a tunnel. The 3931 yard long tunnel opened on 14th October, 1824, and was large enough to take a 60 ton sailing barge of 94'8" length and 22'8" width. In the early days the tunnel became very congested, so much so that in 1830 it was closed to allow for a passing place to be constructed in its centre. The railway age soon began to make its presence felt, however, and in 1844 further alterations were made to allow for both boat and train to share the same tunnel. It was not long before the train won the day and in 1847 the canal was filled in to make way for a double railway track. The canal continued to carry local traffic between Higham and Gravesend until 1920.

Out to the north, on the edge of the Thames marshes, lies the atmospheric and now redundant church of St Mary's. It has a distinctive pattern of alternating bands of flint and stone. The church has been internally rearranged. What was once the south aisle is now the nave and chancel – while the original nave and chancel are to the north. The church is rich in mediaeval fittings. There is a six-sided pulpit from the 14th century. The mighty south door is also from the 14th century. It has similar carvings to a mediaeval four-light window and is enriched with flowers and faces. The delicate perpendicular rood screen is between the original nave and chancel and is of five bays with a central door.

Higham once had its priory – this was sited where Abbey Farm now is to the east of the church.

Cliffe

The church of St Helen at Cliffe stands on an ancient site. Records tell us that Archbishop Theodore of Tarsus summoned a synod of the church here in 673 and "The Clyffe Parish Almanack for 1877" records that between 747 and 824 six councils were held.

The church is often locked, but it is worth finding the key because it is full of interest and has fittings of impressive detail. It is the only church in Kent to be dedicated to St Helen. We are told that she was the daughter of Cole of Colchester – or Old King Cole of nursery rhyme fame – and her son was Constantine the Great. The original church was built in 774 by Offa, King of the Mercians, while the present church dates from the 13th century. The church is elaborately decorated – on the pillars of the nave are appealing chevron markings and there is an ancient tie beam in the nave roof and a pulpit dating from 1636. There are misericords beneath the choir stalls and wall paintings in both transepts. The one on the north shows the Martyrdom of St Edmund. Within the chancel is a gloriously decorated sedilia and piscina with beautifully delicate ogee arches with crockets, finials and pinnacles.

Cooling

The Kent historian, Edward Hasted, wrote of Cooling in 1797: "It is an unfrequented place, the roads of which are deep and miry, and it is as unhealthy as it is unpleasant". It is still unfrequented and the proximity of the marshes makes it a very atmospheric place. The castle is not open to the public, but can be seen quite clearly from the road. Its story begins in 1379, when the menace of French ships sailing up the Thames prompted John de Cobham to apply for a licence to crenellate his home, and so it was that the castle was constructed in 1381 to defend the then important port of Cliffe from the French. The gateway of Cobham's castle is complete and it incongruously frames a modern house behind it. The towers have machicolations and battlements and fixed to the wall is a copper tablet declaring: "that I am mad(e) in help of the cuntre (country)". The castle has two wards separated by a moat.

There are historical associations of a former owner, Sir John Oldcastle, with the Lollards. These were followers of John Wyclif, who taught that the English translation of the Bible should be promoted. Sir John Oldcastle was a fervent follower of Wyclif and, in 1417, was burnt at the stake for heresy after fleeing in vain to Wales. Shakespeare based his character Falstaff on Sir John. The two men were very dissimilar, however, and Shakespeare was forced to retract: "Oldcastle died a martyr and this is not the man".

Cooling castle entered history in Mary Tudor's day. Her marriage to Philip of Spain was not to the liking of Sir Thomas Wyatt who, following his rout of the royalist forces at nearby Strood, bombarded Cooling in 1554. Edward Hasted writes: "Sir Thomas Wyatt marched with six pieces of cannon to the castle, which finding it too strong to take, after having broke down the gate and part of the wall, and having had some discourse with the Lord Cobham, who was in it, he marched next night to Gravesend."

Further along the road is the church of St James. The County Guide recommends these parts for those in need of "space, silence, and solitude". The marshes are desolate and bleak here, and the whole area reminds one of Dickens' Great Expectations. It is said that Pip met the convict Magwitch here and inside the churchyard, just to the west of the south door, lie the thirteen graves of Pip's brothers. The church has ancient 14th century oak benches with Fleurs de Lys poppyhead decoration, and on either side of the chancel are stone stalls (for the weakest go to the wall).

Cooling, like Higham, is under the care of the Redundant Churches Fund.

A unique feature of St James is the small vestry, which is decorated inside with cockle-shells.

Graves of Pip's brothers, Cooling

Grain

People have claimed that Grain is the 'dreariest parish in Kent'. Not a bit
of it. This windswept place has many surprises. It used to be an island –
the Isle of Grain – isolated from the Hoo peninsula by the Colemouth
and Yanlet Creek, but these are now mere ditches. One of the surprises
is that it is real seaside, even for buckets and spades. The place is
windswept and there are fine and extensive views across the Thames to
Southend, across the Medway to Sheerness and beyond to the open sea.
It is the home of what was once the massive Kent Oil Refinery, built in
1950, with its "gleaming metal storage drums" so praised by Pevsner. I
believe it is now a storage depot. Nearby is the enormous Grain Power
Station. This is the largest oil-fired power station in the country and its
five turbines, each of 660 MW, can meet the electricity demand of three
cities the size of Birmingham, Manchester and Liverpool. The site was
used previously, during the First World War, as a marine aircraft
experimental establishment, and before that Queen Victoria is said to
have used the jetties here.

Here industry and nature stand side by side. There are views of the shipping in the Thames and Medway – including the ferry that leaves Sheerness each morning for Holland, seaside, a power station and an oil depot, and not a yuppie in sight! Dreary?

Upnor

There are wide expansive views of the Medway from Upnor, and across the river is Chatham Dockyard. It was for the defence of this dockyard that Elizabeth I first ordered Upnor castle to be built in 1561. The original castle was to the design of Sir Richard Lee and consisted of the main building and the water bastion, which extends out into the river. Later, in 1599, the gatehouse and the north and south towers were added at a cost of £761.9s.10d.

The castle saw action in the second Dutch War. Then, in 1667, under the command of de Ruyter, the Dutch Fleet sailed up the Thames. They destroyed the fort at Sheerness and entered the Medway. A massive chain was placed across the river between Hoo Ness and Gillingham to stop their progress to Chatham. This was fortified by batteries on either side, and all of the English defences were under the command of the Duke of Albemarle. It was all to no avail, for on 12th June the Dutch broke through the chain and burnt several British ships. They also succeeded in capturing the magnificent Royal Charles and sailing it back to Holland. An eight-gun battery just beside Upnor Castle did nothing to deter the victorious Dutch, and the whole sorry episode prompted the diarist John Evelyn to complain of "A Dreadful Spectacle as ever any English men saw and a dishonour never to be wiped off". Upnor's failing was due to its lack of munitions. Pepys, the diarist and Secretary to the Admiralty, wrote "I do not see that Upnor Castle hath received any hurt by them though they played long against it, and they themselves shot till they hardly had a gun left upon the carriages, so badly provided were they".

Following the defeat by the Dutch, the defences of the Medway were reviewed. New forts were constructed at nearby Cockham Wood and Gillingham, and the importance of Upnor declined.

In Dickens' day, prison hull ships were anchored nearby from which Magwitch (whom we met at Cooling) made his escape.

ROUTE

➡ Leave the M25 at junction 2 and join the A2 (signposted Rochester and Dover). Continue for 8.8 miles and turn left for the B2009 (signposted Cobham, Shorne, Higham).

➡ **CYCLISTS: route starts here**

➡ At a T-junction turn right and continue for 1.8 miles to the main A226. Turn right (signposted Rochester). After 0.3 miles turn left into Telegraph Hill at The Sir John Falstaff Inn (711708) (A).

➡ Continue up Telegraph Hill for 0.4 miles, turn left, first right and then immediately right (signposted Higham Station and Cliffe). After 0.9 miles turn right over railway bridge (signposted Strood, Rochester) at Higham station (715727) (B).

➡ At crossroads by Chequers pub, carry straight on (signposted Church Street) for 0.9 miles to Higham church (716742) (C).

➡ Retrace steps for 0.5 miles and turn left into Bull Lane. After 0.3 miles turn left at a T-junction, continue for 0.4 miles and turn left into Buckland Road (signposted Cliffe). Follow the road round to the right after 2.2 miles into Butway Lane and then in 0.3 miles arrive at Cliffe church (736767) (D).

➡ Turn left out of Cliffe church and then first right at the Black Bull pub to Reed Street. After 1.2 miles turn left (signposted Cooling, High Halstow) and continue for 0.6 miles to Cooling Castle (753759) (E).

➡ Continue for 0.1 miles to Cooling church (757759) (F).

➠ Continue through High Halstow and after 3.2 miles, arrive at the main A228. (The route to and from Grain is along a main "A" road and because the attractions of Grain may not appeal to all but the most serious explorer others may wish to continue the route at POINT X by turning left onto the A228 and then turning right after 1.7 miles for the Street(signposted Stoke))

➠ Turn left onto the A228 and after 6.4 miles turn left at Grain fire station into the High Street. Continue for 0.3 miles to sea front (890770) (G).

➠ Retrace steps and turn right at Grain fire station on to the A228. After 4.7 miles, turn left into The Street (signposted Stoke) (POINT X). After 2.5 miles join road coming in from the left and after 0.7 miles turn left. Continue for 2.2 miles (through Hoo) to rejoin the A228, and turn left.

➠ After 0.7 miles keep left at the roundabout for the A228 (signposted Rochester). After 0.6 miles turn left (signposted Upnor). After 0.1 miles turn left into Upnor Road (signposted Upnor). After 0.4 miles turn right (signposted Upnor Castle) and in 0.2 miles turn right for car park at Upnor Castle (758706) (H).

➠ Retrace steps to the A228 and turn left for Strood, where you join the A2 for the M25 and London.

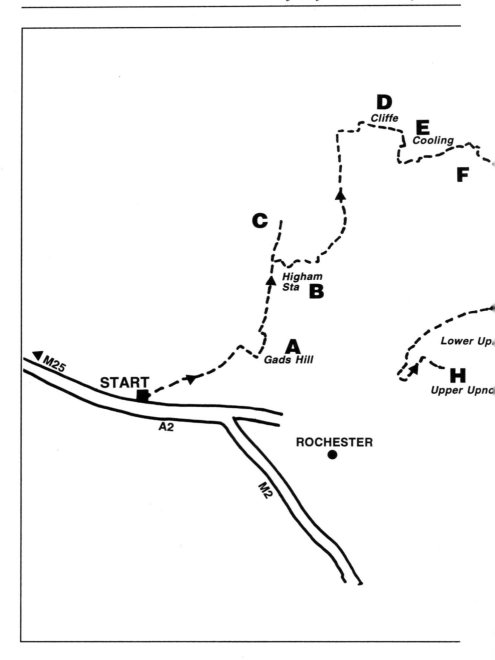

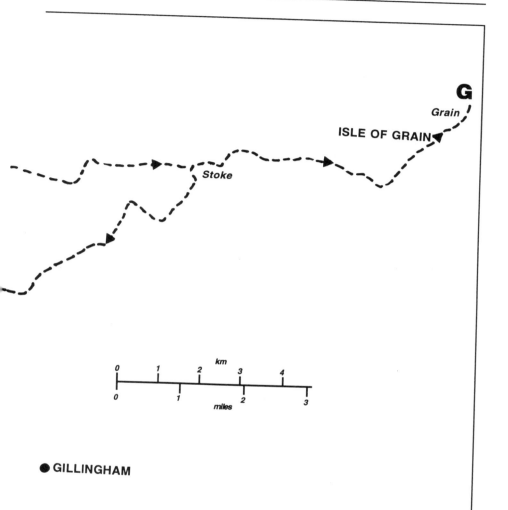

REFRESHMENTS

1. The Sir John Falstaffe – on the main A226 opposite Charles Dickens former home at Gads Hill (711708)

2. The Railway Tavern

3. The Chequers – both by Higham railway station (715727)

4. The Six Bells

5. The Victoria Inn

6. The Black Bull – all in Cliffe village (736767)

7. The Horseshoe and Castle – just past Cooling church (758760)

8. The Red Dog – in High Halstow village between Cooling and the road to Grain (783754)

9. The Cat and Cracker

10. The Hogarth Inn – both in Grain village (886766)

11. The White Horse – in Stoke village by the church (823753)

12. The Five Bells – in Hoo St.Werburgh village (783722)

13. The Tudor Rose

14. The Kings Arms – both in Upnor village (757705)

REFERENCES

Banks, F.R. , *The Penguin Guide, Kent,* Penguin 1955.

Banks, F.R. , *The Penguin Guide, Surrey.* Penguin 1956.

Church, Richard, *The County Books Series, Kent.* Robert Hale 1948.

Collison-Morley, L. , *Companion into Surrey.* Methuen 1938.

Cox, J Charles, *The Little Guide, Surrey.* Methuen 1910.

Cox, J Charles, *Rambles in Surrey.* Methuen 1910.

Cracknell, Basil E. , Portrait of Surrey. Robert Hale 1970.

Fraser, Maxwell, *Surrey.* B.T. Batsford 1975.

Gardiner, Dorothy, *Companion into Kent.* Methuen 1934.

Hearnshaw, F.J.C. , *The Place of Surrey in the History of England.* Macmillan 1936.

Hughes, Pennethorne, *A Shell Guide, Kent.* Faber and Faber 1969.

Jerrold, Walter, *Highways and Byways in Kent.* Macmillan 1907.

Lawrence, Ralph, *Vision of England – Surrey.* Paul Elek 1950.

Mason, Oliver, *South East England.* John Bartholomew & Son 1979

Mee, Arthur, *The King's England, Kent.* Hodder and Stoughton 1936

Mee, Arthur, *The King's England, Surrey.* Hodder and Stoughton 1938.

Nairn, Ian, and Pevsner, Nikolaus, *The Buildings of England, Surrey.* Penguin 1962.

Newman, John, *The Buildings of England, West Kent and the Weald.* Nikolaus Pevsner (ed). Penguin 1969.

Palmer, William, *Wanderings in Surrey*. Skethington & Son.

Parker, Eric, *The County Book Series, Surrey*. Robert Hale 1947.

Parker, Eric, *Surrey Anthology*. Museum Press 1952.

Parker, Eric, *Highways and Byways in Surrey*. Macmillan 1908.

Pitt, Derek, and Shaw, Michael, *Surrey Villages*. Robert Hale 1971.

Spence, Keith, *The Companion Guide to Kent and Sussex*. Collins 1973.

Watkin, Bruce, *A Shell Guide, Surrey*. Faber and Faber 1972.

Wright, Christopher, *Kent Through the Years*. B.T.Batsford 1975.

In addition: Church guides and notes from most of the churches included.

INDEX